HELPING CHILDREN COPE WITH GRIEF

D0060841

Alan Wolfelt, Ph.D.

At Time of Writing:

Doctoral Fellow
Department of Psychiatry
and Psychology
Mayo Clinic
Rochester, Minnesota

Position in 1990s:

Director
Center for Loss and Life Transition
Fort Collins, Colorado

ACCELERATED DEVELOPMENT

A member of the Taylor & Francis Group

Library of Congress Catalog Number: 83-70222

International Standard Book Number: 0-915202-39-5

Publications Coordinator: Cindy Lyons

Associate Editor: Colleen Wolowski

Technical Assistants: Sarah Middleton
                      Neil Young

Printed in the United States of America

For additional information and ordering, please contact:

ACCELERATED DEVELOPMENT
A member of the Taylor & Francis Group
1900 Frost Road; Suite 101
Bristol, PA 19007
1-800-821-8312

DEDICATION

This book is dedicated to three families:

To the memory of my grandparents,
who helped me discover the joy of living
at an early age;

To my parents, Donald and Virgene Wolfelt,
who encouraged and supported me in my growth
into the adult world:

and

To my wife, Carolyn, whose love, friendship,
encouragement, and motivation have given me
the psychic energy required in the preparation
of this book.

FOREWORD

It has been said that we tend to physically avoid the prospect of our own death. We know we will die but the precise time is somewhere in the amorphous future. Thus when I ask my Death Education class of 300 or so students each semester at what age they think they will die, their estimate is significantly older than actuarial tables would allow—that is, if one can elicit a precise age-at-death prediction at all, for many prophesize they will die in "old age" of "natural causes." Rarely is death at age 78 years of chronic leukemia, coronary heart disease, or other specific causes of death.

If it is difficult for us to think about our death, it is my hypothesis that to think of the death of our children is an even greater difficulty. I make the assumption that readers of this volume cherish and love their offspring. We dread the thought of our children suffering pain, dying, and death. Similarly the thought of our children suffering grief is difficult for us to comprehend. As Alan Wolfelt points out, a mythology has been developed. The most common being that young children (say around three years of age) do not understand death or give the death of friend, pet, brother, sister, parent, grandparent, other relative, or Raggedy-Ann doll meaning. They do. Researchers have so indicated.

A body of knowledge exists. In the post-Freud period, Herbert Barry's article, "Orphanhood as a Factor in Psychosis," published in 1936, was among the first publications to deal with children and grief. The drop increased to a trickle with the published systematic research of investigators such as Rene Spitz, John Bowlby, and Al Cain in the 1960s and 1970s. Today the topic is one of legitimate interest, but still no torrent has erupted. As expected, only a few methodologically sound investigations of the meaning given to dying and death by the dying child exist.

Yet, children mourn and children die. Fortunately we have the salubrious choice of preparing ourselves for such crises as best we can. We have the second choice of seeking knowledgeable help when we are unprepared or find our resources overwhelmed by tragedy. This volume by Alan Wolfelt fills a need. As the title indicates, this is a book offering helpful, sound information, suggestions, and activities to those who would understand the vulnerability of grieving children.

Alan Wolfelt is a clinician who has worked with bereaved parents and children. He is an excellent teacher. We had the pleasure of serving together as faculty during the National Death Education and Counseling workshops sponsored by the Forum for Death Education and Counseling. During this time he exhibited his acumen and knowledge as he taught teachers and counselors, both novice and experienced. His presentations then, and his work both then and now, were and are characterized by their timeliness and creativity.

Use this book as you will. Read it straight or pick and choose. As any person somewhat understanding of children would be quick to point out, Helping Children Cope With Grief is germane to more than the topic of grief. It may be considered a valuable tool for parents, teachers, and counselors when their goal is to develop happier, more loving children. Follow Alan's suggestions, always modifying to suit the individual child; and you will, indeed, become a "helping-friend."

July 1983

Dan Leviton, Ph.D.
Professor of Health Education
University of Maryland
Past President, The Forum for
Death Education and Counseling

PREFACE

Humankind will survive only through the commitment and involvement of individuals in their own and others' growth and development as human beings. This means development of loving and caring relationships in which all members are as committed to the growth and happiness of the others as they are to their own. Through commitment to personal growth individual human beings will also make their contribution to the growth and development—the evolution—of the whole species to become all that humankind can and is meant to be. Death is the key to that evolution. For only when we understand the real meaning of death to human existence will we have the courage to become what we are destined to be.

(Kubler-Ross, 1975, pp. 165)

This book is written for parents, teachers, and counselors who have both a desire and a commitment to help children when they experience a death. I am sharing this body of knowledge about children and grief with the aim of assisting "caregivers" in helping children at a vulnerable time in their young lives.

While this book is for parents, teachers, and counselors, the book is about children—about accepting each child as an individual shaped by life experiences. These materials were developed with the belief that each child is deserving of an emotional environment filled with a sense of love, acceptance, warmth, and understanding at a time when the child experiences the death or the loss of someone or something dear. My belief is that the significant emotional experiences of childhood set the stage for how the child evolves a set of expectations, hopes, and methods of relating toward the child's own world. Finally, these materials have been prepared in the belief that we as adults have the capacity to be open, honest, and giving as we help children experience both the joy and the pain that comes from caring deeply for others.

In recent years the desire of parents, teachers, and counselors to learn more about children coping with grief experiences has increased tremendously. Adults want to understand how their own values, beliefs, and behaviors influence children at a time of the death experience. Yet the majority of articles and books written on the subject are directed solely toward a professional audience. A tremendous amount of research findings and discoveries is often buried in the professional journals of the "pure" scientists. In my role as a death educator/counselor, I have found that making these materials accessible and relevant to the people with whom I work is of great importance. Fortunately, an ever-increasing demand is occurring for direct application and relevance in the social sciences, including thanatology. One natural reason for this trend is that we realize that people—be they parents, teachers, counselors, or others—learn more effectively when they perceive how material is related to their own lives and daily experiences. This book focuses on real relationships between children and adults. My desires are to share this information with people who work with children during grief and to have the book be of benefit to my professional colleagues, to parents, and to others who give of themselves to be "helping-healing-adults" to children.

My belief is that any subject becomes more understandable and interesting when it is presented in terms of a number of aspects or dimensions. As a result, I have included a variety of topics aimed at enhancing the adult caregiver's understanding of children's efforts to cope with grief. "Caregiving" is so important that throughout this book caregiving and caregiver each will be treated as one word. Caregiving is an essential element to be received by persons in grief, and especially by children. While these materials in the book, filmstrip, and audio tape are certainly not all inclusive, they are designed as practical resources for adults who are on the front line of emotional care with children at a time of the grief experience of death.

I am grateful to a number of people who have helped make this book and filmstrip possible. First, of course, are the children who have shared their experiences of grief with me and aided in my understanding of what it means to be a child at a time of experiencing grief. I also thank the parents of these children for allowing me to share in their sons' and daughters' young lives. Ken and Doris Parson and Garl Matchett provided me with numerous opportunities to work with grieving children and their familiies. Without these opportunities, this book would not become a reality. A word of appreciation also must be directed toward the parents of young children in Rochester, Minnesota who willingly donated their time to participate in a validation study of a significant portion of the materials contained in this book. In addition, many thanks to those employees of the Mayo Clinic who volunteered to serve as discussion leaders during the implementation phases of the study. Those individuals are David Macy-Lewis, Mary Jane McCarty, Kim Stewart, and Jill Strand.

I also would like to thank the many scientists and practitioners whose research formed the scientific basis of this book. Their efforts have helped evolve a scholarly, yet practical, approach to helping children cope with death. Space prohibits naming all of the people whose encouragement and suggestions have contributed to the birth of these materials, but I wish to assure each one of them of my deep appreciation. Special thanks to participants in my workshops who have helped me to explore and to expand my thinking. I would be remiss if I did not individually mention Dan Leviton, who honored me in writing the Foreword to this book. A tremendous thanks to Dolphus Stephens whose invaluable friendship has had a tremendous influence on both my personal and professional life. He responded with supportive enthusiasm when asked to review the manuscript for editorial suggestions and his guiding hand and heart aided immeasurably in making this book one of hope and help.

I am especially grateful to Joe and Pat Hollis for their unlimited help and understanding in developing this book. A special thanks to my most recent teachers at the Mayo Clinic in the Department of Psychiatry and Psychology; the Forum for Death Education and Counseling; Bernadette Gulassa Kwiatkowski, my photographer; Lucille Herr, my typist; and especially my wife, Carolyn, for being so understanding and supportive during my many absences.

Alan D. Wolfelt

Rochester, Minnesota
August 1983

REFERENCE

Kubler-Ross, E. (1975). *Death: The final stage of growth.* Englewood Cliffs, NJ: Prentice-Hall, Inc.

CONTENTS

LIST OF ACTIVITIES

LIST OF TABLES

LIST OF FIGURES

Chapter **1**

INTRODUCTION

This book is an outgrowth of thoughts and feelings that originated in my childhood. At a very early age I discovered that living involved a continual process of mourning losses. I have come to recognize that our responses to death experiences in adulthood are based upon losses we experienced as children and the models of grief we evolved during this vulnerable time. The early experiences of childhood determine how the child will feel about self and the world, and because coping with loss affects future capacity for intimate relationships early experiences are the foundation on which the child builds a healthy orientation toward life and living.

At age twelve, I first experienced the emotional impact of death. I was away at basketball camp when I received the call that Grandmother had died. During that very day I remember thinking that she really hadn't died. In no way would I accept the thought that I wouldn't make my annual summer visit to her home in Ohio. I really didn't begin to sense the impact of her death until my parents came to take me to the funeral.

Fortunately, my parents allowed and encouraged me to view Grandmother's body at the funeral and to participate in the services. While this experience helped me confront her death, some time had to elapse before I was able to accept the loss. I remember many different thoughts and feelings, like no others, during my childhood. At times I missed Grandma so much that I would imagine myself getting ready to go visit her.

The depth of my feelings of loss ebbed and flowed in the days ahead. At times memory of her faded and I discovered I felt guilty when this occurred. At other times I would discover my parents grieving her death when I was filled with happiness from the day's activities. Once again, I would feel guilty and wonder if I too should be sad for a longer period of time.

What about anger? Oh, how I remember those times when I was angry at the doctor for not saving my Grandma's life! I thought people went to the hospital to get well—certainly not to die! Why couldn't somebody have done something sooner? While I was tempted to direct some of my anger toward Grandma for dying, I found it safer and more comfortable to attempt to keep my anger directed outward. After all, I loved Grandma. I had been taught early in life that you don't get angry with someone you love. This entire experience seemed almost overwhelming at times.

Then there was God. What kind of God would let my Grandma die? My family had gone to church every Sunday since I could remember, so I was having difficulty understanding why God would do such a thing.

Obviously, at times I was confused and isolated in my first experience with grief. Those of us who can remember our own first encounter with death realize that childhood experiences with death can be frightening and lonely. However, if handled with warmth, understanding, and caring, our early experience with death can be an opportunity to learn about life and living as well as death and dying. Fortunately, with the help of loving adults who were willing to admit to some mistakes along the way, I was able to grow to understand the experience of Grandma's death. I also came to understand the importance of allowing children to grieve and to be a part of the family experience at the time of a death.

Our society has undergone a number of changes in its approach to death. This is particularly true with regard to children. In the not too distant past, our society was open and honest about death and children could accept the reality of death. In reference to the drastic changes that have occurred, Gordon and Klass (1979) have written:

> The world in which modern children experience death is different from any child's world of the past. Two trends over the course of this century have influenced and continue to influence the relationship between a child and death. The first is the increasing distance of the immediate experience of death from everyday life. The second is the increasing distance of the child from the adult world. Taken together, these trends have radically changed how a child can respond to death. (p. 5)

Yes, America now has the world's first death-free generation, meaning that now possibly a child may grow into adulthood in the United States and never experience a personal or emotional death in the environment at any time during childhood. We, as Americans, on the average experience death in our family but once in every twenty years. A great number of discoveries in the practice of modern medicine have resulted in the drastic reduction of infant and child mortality and have led to prolonged life expectancy. In the beginning of our century, death was much more familiar to all Americans. When several generations lived in the same household, children at a very young age became aware of the naturalness of the processes of aging, illness, and death. They watched and experienced Grandmother and Grandfather as they grew old in the same home in which children and parents lived. Also the children gathered with other family members when death occurred. The funeral was held in the same home. Children were able to experience tears along with their parents and realize that a significant loss had taken place. Death was something which happened, and because it happened within their own environment, children came to know it gradually, in their own way, and in their own time. Death was not a mystery to the growing child. This exposure and experience at a very young age helped set a stable coping pattern for future experiences.

Today, drastic changes have taken place. Fewer people die at an early age. The child has little experience with the death of relatives because as relatives grow old and become ill, they are oftentimes placed in institutions such as hospitals and nursing homes. Grandparents rarely live in the same household with grandchildren. In addition, hospitals often have strict visitation rules which often exclude children. The result of all this is that the child does not have the opportunity to see the person grow old, get sick, and eventually die.

If we combine the lack of these childhood opportunities with the reality that our society has come to be death-avoiding and death-frightened, we find that the child and the family as a whole often develop difficulty in coming to terms with the grief of a death of relatives or friends. In addition, children of the 1980s are living during a time when we have managed to evolve a lethal technology capable of destroying the world with the flip of a switch. At the same time we continue to strive to enhance the human life span. My thinking is that the present "superficial preoccupation with death" on the part of a number of both professionals and lay people is actually an effort to control one's true sense of helplessness, and may well be a denial of the realistic potential of nuclear death.

Yet, while we as a society attempt to avoid the reality of death, children are confronted at a very young age with situations where they see that life no longer exists: they come upon a dead bird; their pet dog is hit by a car and killed; grandma dies; they watch television where the depiction of a tragic death is a common occurrence; they learn of the tragic murder of children in Atlanta. Questions that children ask about death grow out of these experiences in daily living. Will Mom and Dad die? What happens to dead people? Why do they put dead people in the ground? These and many other questions occupy the developing child's thoughts and feelings. Young children most often turn to adults close to them for help in adjusting to difficult situations and unhappy experiences.

The ability of those adults to be sensitive to and understanding of the young child's actual needs can make the difference in making the experience of death either harmful or helpful to the child's emotional growth. If the child is not given honest answers appropriate to the child's age and level of understanding, he/she may develop some distorted thoughts and ideas concerning the topics of death, dying, and funerals. Because the child's thoughts and fears about death may not be openly expressed, concepts regarding death may become confused and disturbed.

A number of parents have much difficulty in discussing death with their children. When a death occurs, bereaved parents are often so upset by their own loss that they make little, if any, effort to explain to their children what has happened. Many adults attempt to experience life as if death never occurs in the lives of their children. While many children grow into adulthood without experiencing a personal or emotional loss through death, other children do experience a loss. In a school district of 6,000 students Getson and Benshoff (1977) discovered that at least three children die each year and Jones (1977) found that twenty percent (20%) of all students will experience the death of a parent during school years. Children are surrounded by loss from the moment of birth.

When a death occurs, the child senses from reactions of those within his/her life system that something very significant has happened, but often the child does not know what. Parents frequently tell themselves that the fact of death is beyond the child's comprehension and that as parents they can protect the youngster from the anguish they themselves are experiencing. In 1967 Harrison, Davenport, and McDermott demonstrated that adults prefer to distract children from the topic of death and to deny that the children are upset. These authors also observed that our society has never had much in the way of identifiable guidelines to follow in dealing with children's confrontations with death. In that very same year, Becker and Margolin (1967) noted that parents admitted that they avoided the topic of bereavement because they could not bear to face the intensity of their children's feelings. As a result, the child's unwillingness to accept the event of death and to grieve over it is reinforced by the protective attitude of adults.

Parents, teachers, and counselors, by not talking about the reality of death with children, succeed for the moment in postponing reality for themselves as well. So, instead of open and honest answers appropriate to the child's level of understanding and development, half-truths are offered in the hopes that the subject will be dropped.

My experience is that when adults attempt to protect children from physical and emotional effects associated with death of an important person within the family circle, turmoil within both the children and the family often occurs. To want to protect children from all discomfort—physical and psychological—is an understandable wish of the majority of parents. At times children do need protection of some type, however they also need something more than protection. They need adult help in learning to understand and eventually cope with the many emotions of grief. The desire of many adults to "spare children" is often caused by their own feelings of discomfort, fear, or anxiety. In some situations, parents seem to be afraid of how profoundly children will suffer from a death and feel the need to protect their offspring from this suffering. Yet other parents deny that children are real people and behave as if children are too immature to be capable of experiencing a full spectrum of feelings at a time of loss. Instead, these parents often rationalize that children are too young to experience real grief. The all too often result of this is that *the child is caught in the middle, not knowing what he/she should be thinking or feeling. Yes, out of our own doubts and fears we often deprive children of an opportunity to grow through grief and begin to formulate their thoughts about coping with death.*

WHEN SHOULD DEATH EDUCATION OCCUR?

Recently much discussion and a flood of publications have occurred regarding the importance of educating children about death. However, in my thinking, the first step in helping children to cope with the death experience is not through direct-forced education, but rather is through parent education, because they are the primary caregivers. The focus of additional efforts could be on educating teachers, who are without a doubt a fundamental influence on individual development and understanding, and on educating counselors and others with whom the child might come in contact, both before and during the period of crisis.

The most important influence on how children react at the time of a death experience is the response of parents and other significant people in the child's life system. The lack of death education of many parents, teachers, counselors, and other concerned adults caring for children during this time results in the anxieties and fears of a number of well-intentioned people being transferred to the children. Indeed, experience has shown that children often appear to suffer more from the loss of parental support or overprotection than from the intimacy of the death experience itself. The intent is not to prevent the crisis which occurs with a child at the time of a death, but to assist in reducing stress. Also, the intent is to make available caregiving services to individuals so that they can cope in a healthy manner. Even if all stress could be prevented during this crisis period, preventing it certainly would not be the most beneficial, because within the experience itself lies the opportunity for personal growth and enrichment. We as adults must abandon the perception of children as "possessions" and strive to create a collaborative helping-healing relationship. At the same time, if the stress can be kept within reasonable limits, the crisis will be less intense and a better chance for an adaptive response will occur. This is a challenge, and a challenge that must be met.

Education with children should begin before, not after, a death experience. More specifically, death education should occur throughout

Helping Children Cope With Grief

children's development whenever an appropriate "teachable moment" arises. At the same time, adults who wish to be of help to children must first free their own thinking and expand their own awareness toward the need for open and honest communication of thoughts and feelings about death. Until adults consciously explore their own reactions, concerns, thoughts, and fears concerning death, they will find that their attempts to be of help to children during this time will meet with little success.

Yes, limitations do exist as to what adults can do to help children cope with loss; but, certain things can be done. We can help children realize that each is a unique human being, made up of qualities totally unlike anyone else. We can help each develop a positive self-concept—a sense of being able to give love and receive love. And, we can help our children feel glad that they are alive.

The experience of childhood is certainly a special time of life. But during this special time a child should be supported and encouraged by caregivers—be they parents, teachers, or counselors—to discover true self in this world. After all, the child is the most important ingredient in a positive movement toward adulthood.

REFERENCES

Becker, D., & Margolin, F. (1967). How surviving parents handled their young children's adaptation to the crisis of loss. *American Journal of Orthopsychiatry, 37,* 753-757.

Getson, R. F., & Benshoff, D. L. (1977). Four experiences with death and how to prepare to meet them. *School Counselor, 24,* 310-314.

Gordon, A. K., & Klass, D. (1979). *They need to know: How to teach children about death.* Englewood Cliffs, NJ: Prentice-Hall.

Harrison, S., Davenport, C., & McDermott, J. (1967). Children's reactions to bereavement. *Arch's General Psychiatry, 17,* 693-697.

Jones, W. (1977). Death related grief counseling: The school counselor's responsibility. *School Counselor, 24,* 315-320.

Chapter 2

CREATING A CARING RELATIONSHIP: AN OPEN ATMOSPHERE

Children oftentimes suffer more from the loss of parental support than from the death experience itself. Therefore, adults must recognize the importance of creating a caring relationship with children when death is experienced. At times, the loss of a caring relationship with Mom or Dad is added to the child's burden of the loss of another significant relationship.

The child's perception of a lack of caring by parents is frequently misinterpreted to mean that the child is not loved and that parents are not concerned. This oftentimes occurs when parents are in the initial phases of their own grief and, as a result of their own helplessness, feel incapable of providing a sense of security to the child. Instead of a parent blaming self for this phenomenon, it is vital that during these times the parent recognizes this helplessness and provides the child with resources that give a sense of support and understanding.

Illustration: Three days following the sudden death of Tommy's Father, the five-year-old boy asked his Mother, "When is Daddy coming home?" Tommy's Mother was confused and stunned by his question and burst into tears as she withdrew into her bedroom. Tommy was left alone to seek his own sense of understanding in a mass of confusion. Incapable of understanding his mother's response, Tommy may have concluded that his mother's behavior was a rejection of him, when in reality, at an adult level, her response certainly was understandable.

Hopefully, this example illustrates the importance of other familiar and comforting adults being available to young children during such times. While Mother may naturally be incapable of responding on such occasions, other loving adults can be accessible to provide the sense of warmth, caring, and understanding that Tommy needs so desperately at such time. Of course situations will occur where no other adults will be available to the child. In this case parents will need to assure the child that they will talk with him/her as soon as they feel able. Caring adults are capable of emotionally and physically supporting children during vulnerable times in their young lives.

Illustrative Responses. To the example given responses such as the following would be helpful.

Illustration A: When Mother is too upset by her own emotions to talk through the questions, she might respond "Tommy, I know you need to talk about Daddy—and you and I will in just a little bit. Right now I'm too upset."

Illustration B: When Mother is too upset by her own emotions and feels incapable of responding, but is aware that there are other adults available who can provide the sense of security needed at this moment, she might respond, "Tommy, I know you miss your Daddy—I do too. I'm glad Grandma is here to help us both right now." At this point, Mother could see that Grandma could provide Tommy with her comforting presence.

Illustration C: When Mother feels able to follow-through with a discussion with her son, she might respond, "Tommy, I know you really miss your Daddy. You sit on my lap and let me hold you as we talk together."

CREATING AN ATMOSPHERE
FOR CHILDREN'S QUESTIONS

How can parents and other concerned adults create an open atmosphere for children's questions about death? A child's response to the death of loved one is different from an adult's response. This fact alone creates difficulties unless adults are empathetic to the child's grief and are willing to aid in efforts to cope. My experience has been that the child's ability to grieve depends much on what has been learned from parents. Has the child been encouraged to deny or repress emotions or been allowed—even urged—to express feelings of loss, hurt, pain, sorrow, relief, or whatever the emotion may be?

Young children are incapable of grasping all at once what they are being told. However, the information that children gain from the process of questions and answers is often less important than the open atmosphere that such interactions create. Children need to repeat their questions over an extended period of time in order to better understand what is happening or what has happened. They must be given the opportunity to feel directly and indirectly that their questions will be welcomed at any time, and that every attempt will be made to answer them openly, honestly, naturally, and lovingly. As a result, they will gain a sense of security and trust that comes when such truthful information is provided.

Giving children the opportunity to repeat questions enables them to adjust better to the experience of death. The gaining of additional information makes the repeated questions helpful. More importantly the process of repeating the questions aids in the child's healthy adjustment. Each time the child discusses concerns related to death, it becomes a little more bearable. This desensitization of the pain of the death experience is central to the child's adjusting to it. Repeated questions serve yet another purpose. Questions can provide reassurances about parents' interest, concern, and availability. *At times, the questions are asked not so much for the information they provide, but for the opportunity the process of asking them gives the child for involvement with parents.* Parents who are aware of these factors are more likely to be tolerant of children's repeated questions. On the other hand, parents who do not allow for repeated questions will deprive their children of important opportunities to work through reactions to the death in a healthy way. Such questioning by children may continue over a period of weeks, months, or even years. Whenever a child asks a question, the very fact that it has been

The adult-child relationship makes up the principal medium for the child's development of innermost thoughts, perceptions, and feelings which contribute to the reconciliation of the loss experience.

asked indicates that some issue has not been fully resolved. The child who does not ask questions often has been given the message to repress, rather than express, thoughts and feelings.

Unfortunately, at times adults treat children with little respect in their relationships with them. This is reflected in many children's urge to "grow up" so that they can be a "real person." Adult's respect for children is necessary in creating a caring relationship. Validation of the self as a worthwhile person is a need of all humans—particularly children. Adults must be able to respond to that need if they are to be of assistance to children when someone or something dies. Respect and acceptance of the child create a relationship and climate most helpful to the child's growth and self-esteem. The adult-child relationship makes up the principal medium for the child's dealing with innermost thoughts, perceptions, and feelings which contribute to the reconciliation of the experience of loss. Only when the child has experienced a sense of being affirmed will he/she express any doubts, fears, or insecurities to the significant adults in his/her world. As a result, a parent, teacher, or counselor, as a "helping-healing-adult," must create an atmosphere that both verbally and nonverbally communicates to the child that thoughts, fears, wishes, and expectations are to be respected. Respect for the child includes the right to be included in experiences of the family and in the larger community when a death occurs.

CREATING A CARING RELATIONSHIP

Creating a caring relationship involves "helping-healing-adults" sharing thoughts, feelings, values, attitudes, and the interrelatedness among them. The child will experience a sense of respect for unique, individual, and developmentally appropriate responses to death. Perhaps the most important contribution an adult can make in evolving this loving relationship is in the general approach taken with the child. What are some of the important elements that caregivers of children can include in interactions with them? Parents, teachers, and counselors may want to keep in mind the following when striving to evolve a caring relationship: sensitivity and warmth, communication of acceptance, and a desire to understand.

Sensitivity and Warmth

By being sensitive to the perceptions and circumstances of the child, anxieties can be eased. This can be accomplished by taking a phenomenological approach to the helping relationship. This means to focus on each individual child's internal perspective. This "self" theory of helping is based on the belief that children respond in relationship to their self-concept and that their self-concept is for the most part influenced by their experiences with others. This is phenomenologically based in that it is concerned with the child's perception of self and of the situation, not the adult's or the community's perception of the child. If a father loved his son, but the child perceives his father's suicide as dislike and rejection; then for the child, the reality at that moment is that his father disliked him. The caregiver's understanding of this concept is vital to creating a caring relationship with the child.

The adult can further demonstrate sensitivity by being aware of tone of voice, maintaining good eye contact, and being continually aware of what is being not only communicated verbally, but also communicated nonverbally. Perhaps sensitivity is best described as the empathetic understanding of the child, an ability to sense what the child is thinking and feeling. Above all, sensitivity implies love, patience, and the ability to hear and respond to the child's needs.

Parents who continually work on their own self-understanding and awareness are more likely to provide the sensitivity needed to help children during this vulnerable time than those who do not. Parents who are able to separate their needs, feelings, and perceptions from those of their children are better able to evolve the sensitivity and self-understanding that can serve as a basis for helping children develop their own self-awareness. Adult caregivers who are sensitive and self-aware continually ask themselves questions such as:

"How is it that I am feeling this way about my child?"
"What is happening right now?"
"Am I hearing what is being communicated or am I projecting my own perceptions and feelings?" and, perhaps more importantly,
"Is this the child's problem, or my problem?"

Communication of Acceptance

Acceptance means considering the child as a worthwhile person. To assist children at the time of a loss, adults should keep in mind that the goal is to understand the child's feelings and to help, not to judge the child and behavior. Acceptance does not mean approval any more than it means disapproval. Instead, it means that each child is a unique person and deserving of respect and acceptance. The basis of a healthy adult-child relationship is acceptance of the child's right to existence and value. The development of a nonjudgmental attitude toward children when they experience a death in their lives also involves recognizing that at times they will ask questions that may be shocking or seem irrelevant to adults. The ability of the adult to respond to questions without demonstrating shock or embarrassment aids the child in experiencing a sense of empathy and respect.

Related to this nonjudgmental attitude is the acceptance of the child's ability to participate in the decision-making process regarding such matters as attending the funeral, viewing the body, and visiting the grave. The degree to which children are able to exercise this need varies according to age and other factors, but the need is present. This participation is an important part of the growth process in the child's life, a significant part of the adult-child relationship, and a major purpose is aiding children to develop and increase their ability to participate in decision making.

Unfortunately, the right and the need of children to make self-determinations in this area are oftentimes confused because of the social-psychological implications of how our society views death. Adults who give up their own right to decision making at a time of intimacy with death certainly do not model this self-determination behavior for their children. However, the reality of this phenomenon does not limit the existence of this need in children.

Finally, acceptance includes expectation in that adults accept children not only for what they are, but also for what they are capable of becoming.

Desire to Understand

To be effective in helping children cope with loss, adults must convey a commitment to understand. Communication must occur for understanding to take place. In other words, sending and receiving must occur between the adult and the child in the creation of the caring relationship. These communications are intricate, involving a number of behaviors of which the adult is not aware. While the adult will not always understand totally the child's messages, the child usually will sense the adult's desire and effort to understand from both verbal and nonverbal cues. Naturally, the content of the verbal messages is important in communicating understanding.

Nonverbal communication between the adult and child can be a determinant in the helping relationship. Nonverbal communication is constant and is the primary way in which feelings and attitudes are transmitted, particularly at times of family distress. Children are frequently confused by what Virginia Satir (1967) referred to as double-level messages. This is when the adult gives one message verbally and a totally different message nonverbally.

Illustration of Double-level Message. The following is an illustration of a parent sending a double-level message to the child.

Verbal message: "I really want you and me to be able to talk about our memories of Grandpa."

Nonverbal message: Behavior of parent includes moving quickly away from the child and avoiding eye contact even while speaking to the child. The nonverbal message communicated is "I'm tired of your bringing up Grandpa."

Situations like this illustrate a basic rejection of the child's needs. When this occurs, children are perplexed because they do not know which communication is real. This kind of interaction is confusing and often proves to be destructive to vulnerable children. The overall effectiveness of communication is enhanced when sensitive adults are aware of the impact that nonverbal messages have on children.

From the child's perspective, communication involves sending thoughts, feelings, and perceptions either by talking about them or through exhibiting behaviors by which thoughts, feelings, and perceptions can be understood by the helping adult. Simply sending a message does not insure the completion of the communication process. The messages must be received by the helping adult and perceived by the child as being received before the process is complete. "Received" means that the message has been understood by the adult.

Communication, then, involves both the child and the adult—the sender and the receiver. With young children, the lack of language ability often results in an emphasis on the nonverbal, or behavioral, method of communication. Expressions of grief in children are frequently seen in actions, not words. This highlights the need for a desire and a commitment on the part of the adult to understand and search for the meanings attached to a child's efforts to communicate. The ability to understand

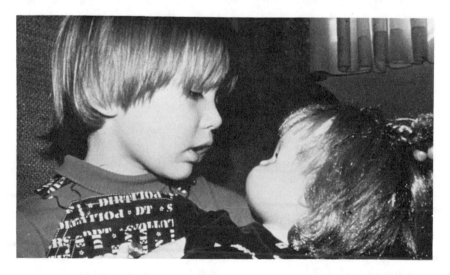

Expressions of grief in children are frequently seen in actions, not words. This highlights the need for a desire and a commitment on the part of the adult to understand and search for the meaning attached to a child's efforts to communicate.

16   *Helping Children Cope With Grief*

meanings depends upon the adult's openness to hear, accurate interpretation of what is heard, and ability to accept the substance of the child's communication.

Desire and ability to understand children do not just happen. The adult must make an effort to establish a very special kind of goal-directed experience with the child. As parents, teachers, and counselors accomplish this, they enhance their ability to empathize with the child, to perceive accurately, and to understand the child's perception of self and the individual experience with death.

In the final analysis, the ability to understand and communicate is to be able to transfer meanings from the child to parent and parent to child. Breakdown in communication is a tragedy and hopefully can be averted by "helping-healing-adults."

REFERENCES

Satir, V. (1967). *Conjoint family therapy.* Palo Alto, CA: Science and Behavior Books.

Chapter **3**

CHILDREN'S UNDERSTANDING AND RESPONSE TO DEATH

(With Caregiver Behaviors)

Yes, we learn much about how children view death by simply listening to them. When children were asked what they thought about death and dying, the following thoughts were expressed:

> Eight-year-old Billy said, "You have to get sick before you die, so I am never going to get sick and I'll never have to die."

> Nine-year-old Judy said, "Only the good people go to heaven. The other people go where it is hot all the time—like in Florida." And

> Ten-year-old Kevin said, "I'm not going to die, because I'm a Boy Scout."

Children's Understanding and Response to Death 19

Parents stand with open arms as their children are born into this world. But as their children grow, respond, mature, and express feelings, many parents fail to welcome them into the adult world. At times, we have to remind ourselves that children are people too. Children do grieve the deaths of those close to them. The experience of loss does not wait for children to grow into adulthood. Even the experience of growing up involves a continued sense of loss in that each time we gain something, we give up something else.

Grief does not focus on one's ability to "understand," but instead upon one's ability to "feel." Any child mature enough to love is mature enough to grieve. Because the very young child has no ability to comprehend the total meaning of death, primarily because of inability at that age to sense time and space, this inability makes the child's response to acute loss potentially more difficult.

In recent years much has been learned about processes and development in the lives of children. This knowledge has facilitated a better understanding of what occurs in the emotional lives of children when they experience in their young life the death of a significant person. For example, at one time it was confidently thought that a young child soon forgets Mother or Father who has died and as a result quickly recovers from any sense of loss. Grief during childhood, it was thought, was short-lived. Now, more specific observations have demonstrated that rapid recovery is not the case and that a child's grief often lasts for a much longer period of time than considered previously.

Professional caregivers have come to realize that people, both children and adults, are always changed through experiences with loss. However, despite the increased attention to the subject in recent years, empirical data regarding how individuals of different ages respond to losses of different kinds and in different circumstances are continually in need of additional research. Perhaps the best we can do for the time being is to draw on the systematic data that are available and make good use of our personal experiences and observations.

Every family and every child are certain to be touched occasionally by "crises" of one type or another and of varying degrees of severity. Some experiences are an integral part of the natural development and growth of the child and the family. Crises of one kind or another are common to all families. However, specific crises are unique to the individual family and child and each "crisis" has meaning for the individual child.

MAJOR FACTORS INFLUENCING
THE CHILD'S RESPONSE
TO DEATH

Providing an opportunity for the child to cope effectively with the crisis caused by the death of a significant person for the most part determines the effect—determines whether or not the death will be valuable in the child's journey of growth and development. The child's capacity to cope with the death depends on many things. The major factors influencing the child's response to death include the following:

- the relationship with the person who has died—the "meaning" of the death;
- the nature of the death—when, how, and where the person died;
- the child's own personality and previous experiences with death;
- the child's chronological and developmental age;

- the availability of family/social/community support; and
- most importantly the behavior, attitudes, and responsiveness of parents and other significant adults in the child's environment.

Caregiving Behaviors

With these general factors outlined one can readily recognize that parents and other loving adults are faced with a threefold challenge in *Helping Children Cope With Grief.* First, adults need to give themselves permission to express their own thoughts and feelings of grief. Giving oneself permission to grieve allows one to eventually move beyond concern for self and to show concern for others. Giving oneself permission also means believing that one is capable of helping the child cope with the grief experience and has enough warmth, love, and sincerity to be capable of caregiving. Permission means not only caring but also giving of self.

Second, adults need to understand the meaning and the effect of the death experience for the child. To understand the meaning is more than hearing the words of the child or making an adult interpretation. Understanding requires a communication between child and adult, a flow of meaningful verbal and nonverbal messages sent and received by each other. A review of the major factors listed previously as influencing the child's response to the loss will aid the adult in working with the child.

Third, adults need to help the child cope with the grief experience. Procedures for doing this are the content of this book.

> *Illustration: Roger's Grandmother whom he loved very much dies suddenly and unexpectedly. What does the death mean to Roger who has spent every summer with Grandmother? What are the Mother and Father's responses to the death experience?*

As previously mentioned, parents' sense of loss, hurt, anger, fear, and a multitude of other emotions often increases the effect of the death experience upon the child. And yet, the way in which parents respond to death—individually, in relation to each other, and with the child—has the potential of making a real difference in the outcome. Consequently, as adults, we often have to remind ourselves that the process is more than finding how to explain but rather involves understanding, experiencing, and coping with our own emotions of grief. We must first become secure enough to give ourselves permission. Once we have satisfied that challenge, we then face the second challenge of sharing ourselves with the child while also helping the child understand his/her own reactions. The third challenge is to help the child cope with his/her own individual experience with the death. All three of these challenges and their resulting behaviors can be done in a caregiving manner that builds emotional stability in both the child and caregiver.

UNDERSTANDING BY AGE LEVELS

For hundreds of years the assumption was that not much occurred in the lives of children until they were old enough to talk or understand what was happening around them. However, we now know that quite the opposite is true. Much occurs that helps to shape the life of a child well before there is any ability to understand or verbalize the meaning of events or behavior in the lives of other persons.

At a very early age children begin to develop some understanding of death. Their perceptions are different than those of adults and children continue to change as they mature and grow. To this date, in a number of studies tremendous variability has been found regarding the specific age at which a mature understanding of death is achieved. This variability appears to be affected by personality factors, socio-cultural factors, prior experiences with death, and probably a multitude of other factors that are unidentified at this point. As a result, we must keep in mind that each child is an individual shaped by experiences of life. With this warning, let us review some major studies of children's age-level perceptions of death.

Probably the two most well known studies completed are those of Nagy (1948) and Anthony (1971). The findings from both studies have been outlined in Table 3.1.

In what is now heralded as a classic study Nagy (1948) noted the following developmental differences in children's reactions to death. In outlining three stages she determined that children, from ages three to five, tend to deny death as a regular and final process. They tend to associate death with sleep or a journey, from which one can return. At this point, the finality of death is not yet recognized. In the second stage, from ages five to nine, children begin to understand the reality of death, yet have difficulty with the thought that they or those around them whom they love will die. In other words, they realize death exists, but they keep it distant from themselves. Nagy's third and final stage is that of a mature understanding. At approximately age nine or ten, children begin to realize the irreversible nature of death and view death as personal. At the same time, they are more inquisitive about biological components as well as aware of social implications of death and loss for survivors.

Unfortunately, this study was completed over thirty years ago in the country of Hungary. How do these findings compare to more contemporary children in the United States? In 1973 Nagy's study was replicated studying children in the United States, who, as compared to the Hungarian children of more than thirty years ago, expressed concepts of death as outlined in Table 3.2 (Melear, 1973).

Stillion and Wass (1979) reported that attempts to replicate Nagy's findings in this country generally have found a relationship between age and breadth of death awareness but have not found the personification of death among six to nine-year-olds that Nagy found. Related to these findings Stillion and Wass made the following astute observation:

Table 3.1

Children's Perception of Death (Nagy & Anthony)

AGE	NAGY (1948)	ANTHONY (1971)
3 to 5	Tend to deny death as a regular and final process. Death is temporary.	Ignorant of meaning of word dead. Limited or erroneous concept of dead.
5 to 9 above	Tend to personify death, to consider it a person. Know death exists but attempts to keep it distant from themselves.	No evidence that children do not understand the word dead. Preoccupied with death ritual.
9 and above	See death as inevitable for all of us. Realistic perception of death.	Understand the word and the event. Define death in biological terms.

Note. Based on "The child's theories concerning death" by M. Nagy, 1948, *The Journal of Genetic Psychology, 73,* pp. 2-37; and *"The discovery of death in childhood and after"* by S. Anthony, 1971, London: Alan Lan, Penguin.

This may lend support to the idea that cultural beliefs and experiences also shape concepts of death. Nagy's children were all firsthand witnesses of a terrifying, bloody war in which death could be delivered from the skies unexpectedly. Most of them undoubtedly lost loved ones during the war. Perhaps it was more natural for those children to make the concept of death more understandable by personifying it. However, these words may also reflect a personification tendency more relevant in Europe than in the United States. (pp. 214-215)

Table 3.2

Children's Perception of Death (Melear)

AGE	MELEAR (1973)
0 to 4	Relative ignorance of the meaning of death.
4 to 7	Death is a temporary state.
	Death is not irreversible and the dead have feelings and biological functions.
5 to 10	Death is final and irreversible but the dead have biological functions.
6 and beyond	Death is final. It is the cessation of all biological functioning.

Note. Based on "Children's conceptions of death" by J. D. Melear, 1973, *The Journal of Genetic Psychology,* 123, (2), pp. 349-60.

In the book *The Discovery of Death in Childhood and After,* Anthony (1971) also outlined three-stage development of children's perceptions of death. She determined that children, ages three to five, are either ignorant of the meaning of the word dead or interested in the word although their concept is limited or erroneous. In her second stage, ages six to eight, no evidence was found of children not understanding the word dead. During this time children appear to be preoccupied with death ritual and define dead in reference only to humanity. Anthony's third and final stage occurs around ages nine to ten, wherein children understand the word dead and the event and define it in reference to biological essentials.

A number of other investigations have attempted to outline various age-level classifications at which specific ideas related to death occur. Outcomes from the investigations lack total agreement on specifics associated with death as determined by the age of the child. However, all investigators do agree that associations move from no understanding toward specifics which is a developmental concept. Thus chronological age of the child is one way of classifying what might be expected in terms of understanding death.

In summary, children appear to proceed from little or no understanding of death to recognition of the concept in the realistic form. While most often stages are listed in chronological order, the individual child may well deviate from the specific age range and the particular behavior associated with that age. While evidence does appear for the age-level-understanding of children's concepts of death, one needs to keep in mind that development involves much more than simply growing older. Environmental support, behavior, attitudes, responsiveness of adults, self-concept, intelligence, previous experiences with death, and a number of other factors have an important role in the individual child's understanding of death.

THE CHILD'S EMOTIONAL
RESPONSE TO DEATH

To aid grieving children, an understanding of the complexity of grief becomes essential. Caregivers ask these questions:

What is grief?
What is death all about?

To aid in answering these questions some semantic distinctions should prove helpful. Therefore, the following definitions are offered:

Death: the event in the child's life that precipitates the emotion of grief. An external event.

Bereavement: state caused by loss such as a death.

Grief: an emotional suffering caused by death or bereavement. Grief involves a sequence of thoughts and feelings that follow the loss and accompany mourning. Grief is a process, and as a result is not a specific emotion like fear or sadness but instead is a constellation of feelings that can be expressed by many thoughts, emotions, and behaviors. Grief is the internal meaning given to the external event.

Mourning: the emotional processes and resultant behavior which come into action following the death of an important person in one's life. "Grief gone public."

Grief Work: activities associated with thinking through the loss, facing its reality, expressing the feelings and emotions experienced, and becoming reinvolved with life.

Several observers have defined models of grief that seem to follow a predictable pattern (e.g., Bowlby, 1973; Engel, 1971; Kubler-Ross, 1969; Lindemann, 1944; Parkes, 1972). However, the majority of models to date have not focused on the grief of children when they experience the death of someone they love. For example, Lindemann (1944) based his model on survivors of catastrophe; Kubler-Ross on observations of the dying; Bowlby on infants; Parkes on widows; and Engel on the chronically ill. These and other authors most typically describe stages as moving from disorganization to reorganization and as moving from shock to recovery.

In my work with children who have encountered death, I have discovered the complexity of their response to require more than the following description that one often hears described:

"Well, first is usually a short period of shock, usually lasting from the time of death through the burial of the body. This is followed by a period of acute grief, where the child may have trouble eating or sleeping, sometimes accompanied by disorganization, withdrawal, and loss of interest in everyday activities. Then there comes a final period of reestablishment, and interests once again turned outward toward life."

I would not disagree with this description, however, my experience has taught me that the child's grief process demands a broader description.

"Helping-healing-adults" must recognize that children express their grief in a number of different ways. Reactions are most often demonstrated in three forms: emotional, physical, and behavioral (Figure 3.1). At times, one form may tend to dominate a child's response; however, one often observes an interrelationship between and within these different forms of response.

My goal is to present a multidimensional model of a child's grief response based upon my experience in working with and observing

Children's Understanding and Response to Death   27

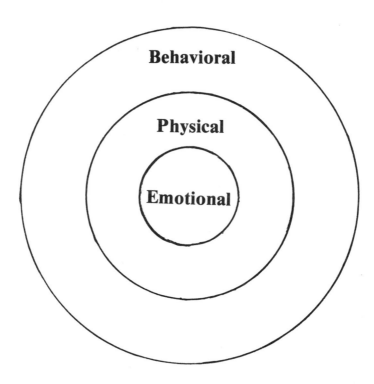

Figure 3.1. Child's reaction to death: three forms (types).

children in their efforts to cope with loss. By no means do I pretend that this model is all-inclusive; however, I do hope it aids the adult caregiver's efforts to assist the child in adjustment to the death of someone loved. I will include a number of separate emotions and feelings frequently experienced by grieving children and include a description of some of the physical and behavioral manifestations as well.

Not every child will experience each and every response described and certainly not necessarily in the order outlined. Some regression may occur along the way and invariably some overlapping. Unfortunately, a child's response to loss is never as uncomplicated as described by the written word.

The responses described are accompanied by somewhat predictable emotions and behaviors. Emotions always find expression and ventilation either in the natural way that is permitted and encouraged or in an unnatural way that is forced. The adult response to loss can be helpful by understanding the child's needs at the different steps along the way.

Ideally, the child's grief moves steadily toward reconciliation. If only this were the case! In actuality, children often work through various phases and then regress to previous phases. During grief, children may well have surges of loneliness and encounter experiences that trigger memories that cut through their exterior to touch emotions both happy and sad. The "helping-healing-adult" must accept the child, not prod, persuade, or entice, but provide opportunities, space, and silences for the child to discuss feelings, or just to be silent in the child's presence. By becoming familiar with and understanding the child's response to loss, the adult is better able to help the child at a most difficult time.

The constellation of thoughts, feelings, and behaviors that have been outlined are based primarily on my counseling experiences with children ages five through twelve. Of course, this does not mean that younger and older children do not encounter many of these same experiences. Prior to outlining this model of grief, a brief summary is provided regarding the very young child (generally before age 4 or 5).

Obviously, the child's response to loss varies with his/her age. The older the child is, the more experiences and personality development he/she has to call upon at a time of loss. Naturally, some children simply by their nature will be more vulnerable, whereas others seem to work through their grief with little difficulty.

How many times have you heard a statement similar to the one made in the following illustration?

Illustration: The six-year-old son of a family was killed by a hit-and-run driver. In the family was a younger three-year-old daughter, Karen. When a neighbor was talking with the mother soon after the accident, the mother commented, "I don't think I'll tell Karen anything, she's really too little to understand."

Perhaps so, but not too young to feel and respond at her own level.

Even if a young child has no language with which to communicate, this child is not prevented from both experiencing and expressing feelings. Parents certainly communicate with their child from the moment of birth. Because the young child's being is so tied to feelings, the result is a sensitivity to the feelings of surrounding persons that is probably never recaptured later in life. If a change occurs in the emotional atmosphere, the child senses it. When the loss is of a person who is warm, giving, and loving, the child realizes it. The nurtured world and the child's sense of security are threatened in a very powerful way. The child may well respond to changes by becoming physically ill, refusing to eat, withdrawing emotionally, or being easily agitated. *The emotional meaning attached to the event of loss early in life becomes a part of the child forever, regardless of the ability to remember the specific event.*

Caregiving Behaviors

In responding to needs of the young child, the caregiver must provide an emotional sense of comfort, love, warmth, attention, and acceptance. In other words, the process of helping the child cope with the loss demands a "helping-healing-adult" who can provide the emotional support and care necessary.

A young child with no language with which to communicate is not prevented from both experiencing and expressing feelings. If a change occurs in the emotional atmosphere, the child senses it, the child realizes it—the child's sense of security is threatened.

DIMENSIONS OF CHILDHOOD GRIEF
AND CAREGIVING BEHAVIORS:
A MODEL FOR ACTION

Caregivers need to be aware of the means by which children express grief. In accepting dimensions, recognizing them for what they are, and learning caregiving behaviors a caregiver is *Helping Children Cope With Grief.*

To place dimensions into a manageable framework, thirteen (13) dimensions have been identified. These thirteen dimensions, typical of what frequently is exhibited by children experiencing grief, are listed in Figure 3.2. The balance of this chapter is devoted to discussion of these dimensions.

RECONCILIATION
LOSS/EMPTINESS/SADNESS
RELIEF
GUILT AND SELF BLAME
FEAR
ACTING OUT BEHAVIOR
EXPLOSIVE EMOTIONS
DISORGANIZATION AND PANIC
"BIG MAN" OR "BIG WOMAN" SYNDROME
REGRESSION
PHYSIOLOGICAL CHANGES
LACK OF FEELINGS
SHOCK/DENIAL/DISBELIEF/NUMBNESS

Figure 3.2. Dimensions of childhood grief.

Many well-intentioned adults might find themselves attempting—consciously or unconsciously—totally to prevent the expression of any number of these aspects of childhood grief. Such a goal is most often self-defeating, in that such attempts often cause one not to be as accepting of children's natural expression of a number of thoughts, feelings, and behaviors. In addition, many adults—knowingly or unknowingly—punish themselves for not having prevented such expression.

Children's experiences with the death of someone they love can and often does produce major emotional, physical, and behavioral changes. Fortunately, caregivers can help children cope with these changes while at the same time learning and enhancing growth.

SHOCK/DENIAL/DISBELIEF/NUMBNESS

Often a child's initial response to the death of someone they love is a sense of emotional shock. In this shock the child may say or think, "No, this didn't happen. Daddy's not dead. He'll come back." Or, "If I pretend this isn't happening, then maybe it won't be." The mind is blocking and at times is not connected to listening. There is a gap between the child's thinking and emotions. In reality, "shock" is a generic concept that involves a combination of emotions as well as a physiological component (see section in this chapter entitled "Physiological Changes"). The sense of disbelief the child experiences is beyond logical thinking on the child's part. Many children grow to discover that there are no adequate words to describe this initial period of grief.

On occasion, outside observers jump to the conclusion that disbelief means total and complete denial of the death. However, with responsive guidance children are able to allow enough reality through, according to their own needs, to pace their experience; whereby they move toward their grief instead of away from it, if they are allowed to do so. When reality seeps through, in this sense of disbelief, children may well do some "catch-up grieving" as thoughts and feelings surface that previously have been blocked from full consciousness.

A cardinal difference exists between adults' respecting the naturalness of the denial mechanism and adults' inappropriately encouraging the child to suppress other emotional responses. It is cruel to reinforce a child's belief that Dad will come home when we realize this is impossible. Statements like "Be strong," "You shouldn't cry," and "Well, now you will have to carry on," often encourage the suppression of emotions and as a result reinforce a prolonged sense of denial. At times, adults' difficulty in explaining the finality of death to children results in confusion as to what to think or feel.

This experience of shock, denial, disbelief, and numbness is typically most intense during the six- to eight-week period immediately following the death of someone loved. However, to see this dimension of the child's grief recur suddenly is not at all uncommon, particularly on the anniversary of the death or on other special occasions (birthday, Christmas, etc.) I also have witnessed this dimension when the child visits a place associated with a special memory of the dead person.

Caregiving Behaviors

The major role of the adult caregiver during this shock/denial/disbelief/numbness time is to keep the grieving child in touch with a supportive, caring part of the world. The acceptance of the naturalness of this temporary protective mechanism is an important step in coping with grief.

LACK OF FEELINGS

One of the more difficult dimensions of a child's grief for adults is what may appear to be a *lack of feelings.* Parents often have difficulty understanding how the child can be out in the backyard playing only an hour after learning of Grandfather's death. Yet, what may seem to be the child's lack of feeling is frequently the child's attempt to protect self in the only way known. This apparent inability to feel is often tied closely to the sense of denial and disbelief and once again is a normal manifestation of the child's grief response.

Parents frequently feel hurt and angry with the child's apparent "indifference" and as a result parents end up distancing themselves from the child. This experience can be reframed for parents by recognizing that the child is actually finding grief too much to accept right now and is responding in the only way known.

What can be so confusing to the child is that in some respects this lack of feeling is viewed as a positive response by some in our society who advocate facing trauma without showing feeling. The person who doesn't cry when someone dies is most often the one whom others believe "took things so well." So, while the child receives this message from some adults, others simply can't understand why the child is not grieving and ask themselves if the child really loved the person who died. The result is that the child is frequently stuck in the middle not knowing what to think, feel, or do.

Caregiving Behaviors

Major roles of adult caregivers during the lack of feelings dimension of grief are to do the following:

1. recognize the naturalness of this response,

2. be careful not to punish the child in both direct and indirect ways, and

3. be aware of double-messages the child sometimes receives and prevent such messages from occurring.

PHYSIOLOGICAL CHANGES

A child's body responds to what the mind has been told at a time of acute grief. Among the more common somatic behaviors exhibited in childhood bereavement are the following, classified in Figure 3.2 as physiological changes:

• tiredness, lack of energy;
• difficulty in sleeping or on other occasions prolonged sleeping;
• lack of appetite or excessive appetite;
• tightness in throat;
• shortness of breath;
• general nervousness, trembling;
• headaches;
• stomach pain;
• loss of muscular strength; and
• skin rashes.

In the majority of situations, adult caregivers can help the grieving child recognize that the majority of responses are quite normal and temporary, thereby lessening some of the concern over these symptoms. At times, children unconsciously assume "sick roles" in an effort to legitimize their feelings to others. Unfortunately, this often occurs when the child does not receive permission to express thoughts and feelings in other ways. With little or no outlet to express feelings in a natural way, the child expresses feelings through physical being. One also should be aware that physical disorders present prior to the loss tend to become worse. In addition, it is not unusual to witness a child identify with the physical symptoms that have caused the death of the person loved. For example, if Dad died of a heart attack, the child may complain of chest pains.

Caregiving Behaviors

Adults must be understanding of physical changes that may occur in the bereaved child. Dependent on the extent of the symptoms, consulting a medical doctor may be necessary to rule out physical causes for the symptoms. Helping the grieving child to understand physical symptoms as a normal facet of grief often allows these symptoms to lessen as the child progresses through the work of grief. For further discussion of physiological changes and caregiving behaviors, see Chapter 6.

REGRESSION

Under the psychological stress of grief, children frequently wish to return to the sense of protection and security they have experienced at earlier points in their life. In responding to the sense of loss experienced, normally the child will want to return to an earlier developmental level. In reality, even adults often desire the protection of a parental-like figure during times of stress. Unfortunately, our society often perceives regressive behaviors as a total lack of self-control and discourages or punishes both adults and children for displaying this type of behavior. When experiencing acute grief, strength really lies in accepting natures way of responding as a simple human who is being self.

Among the more common regressive behaviors of childhood bereavement are the following:

•Over dependence on parent to point of declining to go outside to play as they have in the past;

   •a desire to be nursed or rocked as they were at an earlier stage of development;

•a desire to sleep with parent;

   •an inability to separate from parent for any length of time;

•request others to perform tasks for them that they were previously able to do for themselves, for example, tie shoes, dress themselves, feed themselves, ask to be carried, and so forth;

•refusal to work independently in school setting and/or demand constant individual attention and demonstrate dependent seeking behaviors to teacher and peers;

•taking on of a "sick role" in effort to avoid attending school;

•regression to talking "baby talk" and in general presenting themselves in an infant-like manner; and

   •breakdown in ability to function adequately in peer relationships.

Typically, regressive behaviors in bereaved children are temporary and pass as the child is supported in the journey through grief. The caregiver's understanding of the natural and temporary nature of the child's regressive behaviors allows for a sensitive response to the child's needs at this step in the grief process.

When regressive behaviors continue for long periods of time, other factors may complicate the child's response. On occasion parents or other significant persons in the child's life actually reinforce or encourage the regressive display of behavior. Because of the subjective nature of the trauma of adult's own grief, they sometimes feel they are neglectful of the child's needs. In an effort to reduce their own guilt, adults attempt to compensate for this either real or false sense of neglect by overprotecting or overindulging the child. The consequence of this action is that the child may be kept in a dependent position as a result of the parents' need to feel in control of both the child and the situation.

> *Illustration: A mother finds reasons for daughter, Alice, to stay home for two months after Alice's father's death. The stay at home made it impossible for Alice to take part in peer activities and impossible to continue her growth in normal, healthy ways. While the mother may have felt that she was setting restrictions on Alice out of concern, the mother may well have been doing*

this out of a sense of guilt, a need to control, or, as I have witnessed on a number of occasions, to protect the parent from being alone.

This fear of being alone on the part of parents is most often related to their own grief and at times manifests itself in a smothering-like dependence on the child. In many ways, each time parents care for children, parents feel as if they too are receiving care. More specifically, the need to care for the child is a consequence of parent's own felt sense of a need for care. This occurs more frequently in families that have few outside support systems beyond the family.

These regressive behaviors described can take place at anytime during the process of grief; however, they tend to be demonstrated to a greater extent immediately following the death. Typically, I view prolonged regressive behaviors as a barometer of emotional needs that are either not being met in a healthy, loving manner or, on the other hand, are being encouraged by adults in an effort to meet their own needs.

Obviously, regressive behavior indicates stress and the potential need for helpful intervention. Temporary regression undoubtedly serves a useful purpose for many children and is an appropriate response. Sensitive caregivers who recognize prolonged regressive behavior as a cry for help can intervene to assist the child in the grieving process.

Caregiving Behaviors

The caregiver who is attempting to assist the child who demonstrates prolonged regressive behaviors will want to keep in mind that the focus of helping should not be on trying to repress the symptoms but on understanding and reducing the specific contributing factors. Regressive behaviors may be in socially accepted forms. The caregiver must recognize and accept the behavior while reducing the contributing factors.

> *Illustration: Mike, an eleven-year old, experienced the death of his mother two months ago. Now Mike makes statements to his father such as "Please don't go to work today." "Please don't leave me here, I want to be with you." "Daddy, why don't you stop smoking?" "Do you feel all right?" "Did you get enough sleep last night?"*

As in the illustration, bereaved children often display regressive behavior based on the fear that a surviving parent or another significantly loved person in their life also will die. In this situation, both reassuring and demonstrating that the surviving parent is in good physical health and is there to support and care for the child will help in lessening regressive symptoms.

"BIG MAN" OR "BIG WOMAN" SYNDROME

The opposite of regressive behavior on the part of the bereaved child is what I refer to as the the "Big Man" or "Big Woman" syndrome. This is when the child attempts to grow up very quickly and to become the "man or woman" in the house, often in an effort to replace the dead parent.

> *Illustration: Amy's mother died six months ago. Amy and her father have been working through their grief. However, Amy's father said to a friend, "My daughter Amy, who is only ten years old, tries to be just like her mother was. She has been trying to cook all of the meals and insists that she sits where her mother did at the kitchen table..., she cleans the house in the same order and manner of my wife..., she waits at the door when I return from work and asks me about my day in exactly the same words my wife used for years."*

This attempt to take on an adult-like role similar to the parent who has died is often a symbolic way of attempting to keep the person alive. Or, it could be another way for the child to attempt to protect self from a sense of hopelessness and helplessness that may be felt at some point during grief. The child may well try to use words that the parent used and take on a number of roles previously held by Mom or Dad. Frequently the child attempts to care for and discipline other children in the family. Unfortunately, this forced sense of maturity on the part of the child is at times reinforced by adults who may well feel overwhelmed themselves and find it easier to respond to the child at this inappropriate level. The surviving parent may actually consciously or unconsciously attempt to have the child replace the dead parent and, as a result, a sense of confusion and uncertainty will be created on the part of the child.

Caregiving Behaviors

An awareness by adult caregivers as to the potential of the "Big Man" or "Big Woman" syndrome occurring can aid in the prevention of this behavioral manifestation on the part of the bereaved child. When it does occur, an understanding of contributing factors will assist in permitting and encouraging the child to follow as normal a maturational developmental pattern as possible.

DISORGANIZATION AND PANIC

A dimension of childhood bereavement that often occurs suddenly and unpredictably is a heightened sense of disorganization and panic. A wave of overwhelming thoughts and feelings leads the child to ask, "Who is going to take care of me now? Will our family survive? Will I survive?" Fighting against the reality of the death, the child experiencing grief often questions if something is wrong. At times children may feel as if they are out of touch with the ordinary proceedings of life. The dimension of disorganization and panic is prevalent during this time, and many children become frightened at the length and intensity of their feelings.

During the disorganization and panic dimension the child often confronts both good and bad memories from the past. While the child receives comfort from remembering the sound of Mom's voice, it is also painful. And then at other times the child wants to remember experiences and memories of the past and finds doing so impossible. While this loss of memory is normal, it can be very scary to the child who doesn't understand it.

During this phase of grief the child may dream of the parent who died, may appear restless and irritable, may appear unable to concentrate, or may experience a disruption in normal eating and sleeping patterns. The child may seem hypersensitive and cry over what may seem totally unrelated to the grief.

Caregiving Behaviors

This dimension of disorganization and panic for the child tends to peak during the period of time from one month to six months following the death of a significantly loved person. The primary need of children during this dimension of their grief is for the constant physical presence of someone they can trust. Often a real need exists for physical contact (hand-holding, hugging, caressing) to assure them of the caregiving that is and will be extended to them. They need to be reassured about the naturalness of their feelings and behaviors during this period of grief which in other circumstances would be considered highly unusual. During this time the child may have a real need to cry and talk for varying periods of time. The role of the adult caregiver is not to interrupt with false reassurances, but to let crying and talking take their natural course. At times the content of what the child may be saying may seem to make little sense; however, what the child is doing can be quite helpful and clarifying for the child. In moving through and being supported during these frightening dimensions of grief, children are capable of turning grief into growth and pain into gain.

EXPLOSIVE EMOTIONS

The explosive emotions dimension of grief is often the most upsetting for adults in the environment of the grieving child. The reason is the uncertainty of how to respond to the child's expression of these complex emotions. Explosive emotions like anger, hatred, and terror all have their distinctive features. However, adequate similarities exist in the child's underlying needs to warrant discussing the various explosive emotions together.

Explosive emotions may be manifested in several different ways among bereaved children. The child may be angry at the person who died because as the child views the situation, "If Mom had loved me enough, she wouldn't have died and left me." Then the child may reason "If Mom doesn't love me, no one can love me. There must be something about me that makes me unlovable." Or the child may feel that if the person took better care of self the death could have been prevented. Anger and rage may be directed toward anyone: physician, pastor, friends, God, or the world in general. Children may ask themselves if they should ever love anyone again, thinking that another person they love also may "die."

Illustration: Twenty-six-year-old Jim, who was eleven when his Father died, expressed the following: "At first I was really angry

*at Dad for causing me so much pain and for leaving me alone to
cope with life. At times I thought he died because he didn't care
about me. For awhile I blamed the doctor for not saving him. Of
course, I thought Mom should have known something was
wrong with Dad and prevented his death in some way. And then
I went through a time when I was angry at myself for all those
times when I hadn't done what Dad asked me to do...or I'd get
angry at myself for the times I had expressed anger toward Dad
and wished he would go away and leave me alone. It all got very
confusing at times. There was no way I could express anger
toward God outwardly because nobody in my church or family
would allow it...but I sure did feel it. There were those times
when I was angry and didn't think I should be and I would end
up feeling down on myself. I even got mad at my best friend
because he still had a father and I didn't."*

This example helps illustrate that behind these explosive emotions
are the child's more primary feelings of pain, helplessness, frustration,
and hurt. The adult caregiver needs to be in touch with these primary
feelings, recognizing that they often will be expressed in the form of explosive emotions. Adults who attempt to repress the child's anger often
deprive the child of the value of explosive emotions as a means of
psychological survival. Unfortunately, some children are taught that to
"be good" means that one never expresses anger regardless of circumstances.

Caregiving Behaviors

Adults must be careful not to induce feelings of guilt in children
over the wide spectrum of explosive emotions they may express. Anger is
a natural part of grief, and we as adults can help children by accepting
their feelings and not punishing them when they express anger. During
this time the adult caregiver may well be used as a whipping post by the
child. Through permissive listening, the bereaved child learns that feelings are not judged as being good or bad, but are accepted as being real
and present. A real need at this point is for adults in the child's life to be
accepting of all feelings and to create an understanding that such strong
and strange feelings are natural and eventually will subside.

Some children may turn their anger inward and become deeply
depressed, withdraw, develop prolonged physical symptoms, or become
violent and unmanageable. If this behavior persists over time, professional help may be needed.

ACTING-OUT BEHAVIOR

Some children express the pain of grief through acting-out behavior. The specific acting-out behavior usually varies depending on the child's age and developmental level. The child may become unusually loud and noisy, have a temper outburst, start fights with other children, defy any authority, or simply rebel against everything. Often the child's grades drop at school, he/she may begin to associate with a different group of friends, and older children may run away from home. Bereaved children do feel a sense of deprivation and some of them will act-out their anger.

As written previously, bereaved children often feel as if their dead parent has abandoned or "died on them." Consequently they may feel unloved and have a very low sense of self-esteem.

Illustration: Twelve-year-old Brad stated shortly after his mother's death, "Why should I stop fighting at school and causing trouble in class? There is nobody around anymore who really cares about me."

This kind of thinking often leads children to reject others with antisocial behavior, the kind that will keep themselves from any close relationships and the possibility of being "abandoned" again.

Caregiving Behaviors

Again, an understanding of the underlying factors that may be contributing to the child acting-out behavior is vital to the helping process. Parental lectures to bereaved children about acting-out behavior are usually not very productive. Instead, one must attempt to grasp the emotional root of the behavior and attempt to meet the child's needs for affection and a sense of security. Being overly lenient with a child because a significant person in the child's life has died often only makes the acting-out behavior worse. Frequently, bereaved children need and indirectly ask for specific limits as a means of reassurance that they are loved and that someone is giving the protection, the attention, and the caring they need.

FEAR

A child coping with death and the grief process often experiences fear. When the reality begins to set in that the parent or other significant person in the child's life will not be coming back, it is not unusual that the child becomes frightened. During these times children may ask themselves: "If one parent dies, will the other? Daddy left me, will Mommy do the same?" Frequently underlying this commonality is the fear that there will be no one to take care of them. This fear often is increased when the child witnesses a surviving parent struggling with his/her own grief. The parent may seem detached from the child's world and appear incapable of caring for the child. Related to this experience is the child's fear of watching people whom they love grieve. The capacity of parents and other adults surrounding children to reassure them that they are loved and will be cared for is vital during this time.

Another common fear of the bereaved child is the fear of ever loving again. The child may reason that if they had not loved the dead person so much, that then they would not be experiencing the pain of this grief.

> *Illustration: Debbie, twelve-years-old, experienced the death of her Mother five months ago. Now she attempts to create a distance herself and others. Through her behaviors she sends to others the message, "Stay away, don't get too close. If I allow myself to love you, you may die too."*

Helping children understand and accept these feelings will help them cope. Children can be helped to understand that giving and receiving love are two of the greatest gifts of life. Often children have difficulty understanding that the pain of grief is part of life, living, and loving. However, the presence of caring adults can make a true difference in the child's coping with his/her many fears.

Another common fear that many bereaved children appear to experience is the fear of their own death. They may express fright at the slightest hint of illness or secretly feel that they too will soon die. Again, the child needs reassurance and the loving support of surrounding persons.

Caregiving Behaviors

Loving adults must train themselves to be sensitive to a child's fears. For example, children's questions related to an adult truly caring about them are frequently an attempt to determine if they can count on the adult not to leave physically or to die. Accepting children's questions and fears means you accept each child, and the child is extremely sensitive to the slightest hint of rejection during the time of grief. Also recognize that underneath expressions of fears is the emotional need for warmth, acceptance, and understanding.

GUILT AND SELF-BLAME

A very human act for both adults and children is to think and bring about self-blame at a time of death. For children this action can be a difficult struggle because children have particular difficulty in understanding cause-and-effect relationships. Young children often believe that thoughts cause actions; they believe that by thinking about something they can make it happen. Most children have wished their parents would go away and leave them alone at some point. So when the parent dies, the child may well assume blame for thinking these thoughts and as a consequence feel guilty. The child may blame self for any number of things, ranging from being bad to having had angry feelings toward the person who has died. The child may take total responsibility for the death, yet say nothing to anyone about this feeling. If adults are not perceptive and aware of this phenomenon, it may well go unnoticed.

The dimension of guilt may be revealed when the child makes statements to self such as "If only I would have...," or "I wish I could have...," or "Why didn't I ..." Self-defeating thoughts and behaviors often mount as the grieving child experiences feelings of guilt. Frequently interrelated to feelings of self-blame is the child's sense of helplessness and worthlessness. The child may say to self: "I am a bad person for what I have done or not done." Children often feel that they will be punished in some form and may actually seek out forms of self-punishment. This sense that something bad will happen may become a self-fulfilling prophecy.

When children feel helpless, they may attempt to gain some sense of control by thinking that if they would have done something differently, the person they loved would not have died. In other words, if they see themselves as being the cause, they think there may well be something they could do to bring the person back to life. The child may say to self or others: "If you come back I'll be good, I'll never be noisy again or make you get up early with me." This kind of thinking is at times reinforced in those families where someone else is always to blame for whatever happens.

Caregiving Behaviors

How does a "helping-healing-adult" respond to a child's feelings of guilt and self-blame? Foremost, provide opportunities for the child to talk in a realistic fashion about the person who has died. Avoid behaviors that might reinforce the thought that death is a form of punishment. As the child recalls memories, either good or bad, talk about them openly and honestly in an effort to help the child understand that being angry or upset with a person does not cause the person to die. The child can be helped to understand that it is normal for people to get angry at times with those people about whom they care. The bereaved child also can be helped to understand that one cannot control certain things in life.

In the case of the child who is too young to articulate thoughts and feelings, the sense of a trusting relationship with an adult figure is paramount. Adults are capable of expressing a sense of warmth and acceptance through nonverbal as well as verbal means. Just as children learn to be able to give love by being loved, they learn self-acceptance by being accepted. For the verbal child the opportunity to participate in a permissive, patient, and nonjudgmental relationship often allows for the opportunity to work through feelings of guilt.

RELIEF

The bereaved child's expression of a sense of relief is an emotion that is frequently overlooked by adults surrounding the child. Relief is natural after experiencing a long illness of a person who is loved. This is simply a part of being human and yet unfortunately many children struggle with this emotion without an understanding of its naturalness.

At times children are not permitted to express any sense of relief. The lack of permission often is caused by adults who unknowingly encourage the repression of such emotions. As a consequence, relief is very difficult to admit. It is equally difficult to make the adjustments that result from the relief. When adults do not allow and therefore do not help the child anticipate this emotion, the result is often feelings of guilt. The child may think he/she is the only one involved in the event of death who experiences such feelings. The result is all too often a tremendous self-imposed attack on the child's self-esteem, when in reality it is very natural to be relieved both for the person who has suffered a prolonged, painful death as well as for oneself.

Caregiving Behaviors

The caregiver can help the child anticipate the relief emotion as well as listen acceptingly without implying or increasing any feelings of shame or guilt. The child has a real need for the expression of these feelings of relief. Relief certainly does not imply a lack of love for the dead person.

LOSS/EMPTINESS/SADNESS

This dimension of grief is often the most difficult for bereaved children. The full sense of loss and emptiness never takes place all at once. As the full sense of loss begins to set in, sadness, emptiness, and depression often follow. These dimensions are often at the point when the child realizes that the person will not be coming back. This sense of loss and emptiness may take place long after support is thought to be necessary. While dependent on a number of factors, a child might typically experience this dimension of grief six to ten months following the death. Children may wonder why they are crying more at this time than they did just after the death occurred.

As children struggle to come to terms with the finality and reality of the death, they very naturally become depressed in their response. The death of a significant person in their life is something about which to be depressed. During this time the child may demonstrate:

- •a lack of interest in self and others,
- •change of appetite and sleeping patterns,
- •prolonged withdrawal,
- •nervousness,
- •inability to experience pleasure, and
- •low self-esteem.

The child may feel totally alone and empty with the consequence that these feelings usually heighten.

The child who is not in an environment conducive to recognizing and encouraging loss, emptiness, and sadness will sometimes be in the position of being in conflict about expressing these feelings. Suppressed feelings often push for release, while the child is encouraged to repress them. The frequent result is increased anxiety, agitation, and a sense of being emotionally and physically drained.

Obviously, the bereaved child is particularly vulnerable during this period of time. The child may actively seek a substitute for the person who died. Feelings of attachment can be displaced to the extent that a strong dependency upon another person occurs. The person to whom the child attaches him/herself often reminds one of the person who died.

Caregiving Behaviors

The frequent and regular presence of a supportive and stabilizing adult caregiver is helpful during the dimension of loss/emptiness/sadness. While becoming involved in strong new attachments on the surface may appear to be helpful to the child at this time, continuing the work of grief is really the task at hand. The child should be encouraged to talk about intense feelings. An important person in the child's life has died, but that person still exists in the memory of the child. The child should not be denied the opportunity to express these feelings and work them through.

At times, children find it easier to express such intense feelings through play, art work, or writing. Whatever helps the child to express and explore feelings should be respected. One should not be surprised that if during this dimension of the child's grief the child appears to review the events preceding the death and the death itself. It is as if each time the child talks about the death it becomes a little more bearable.

To help the child during this time, the adult must recognize that one's own memories of death and the dead person will be triggered. One has to be careful not to shut off the child's grief in an effort to protect one's own emotions. Modeling the expression of feelings to the child is often a very effective permission-giving tool to assist the child. For example, the adult might say something like the following: "Sometimes I feel really sad and lonely when I think about..." This type of communication lets the child know that these feelings are not so strange and that they need not be embarrassed or afraid to talk about them.

The child is aware of the emotional environment. Caring adults are capable of communicating to children in both word and touch that they are not alone in their grief. Children always will have memories of the person who has died. Children also must be helped to move in the direction of being capable of encountering life, living, and loving once again.

Adults should avoid using specific timetables with specific points at which a child should "be over" grief. Reconciliation is not a process of "getting over" grief or "forgetting" memories, but rather is a process of coming to terms with grief and memories.

RECONCILIATION

The final dimension of grief in a number of proposed models is often referred to as resolution or recovery. This dimension often suggests a total return to "normalcy" and yet in my experience everyone—adults and children alike—is changed by grief. To assume that life will be exactly as it was prior to the death is unrealistic and potentially damaging. Resolution or recovery is often seen erroneously as an absolute, a perfect state of reestablishment.

Reconciliation (a term I believe to be more expressive of what occurs) is achieved when a whole and healthy person emerges from grief. This person at the same time recognizes that life will be different without the presence of the significant person who has died. The bereaved child's *reconciliation after a death is a process, not an event.* Reconciliation never occurs all at once and is often a slow and painful process. The intensity and length of a child's grief must be understood in terms of the life relationship with the person who has died. (Adults should avoid using specific timetables with specific points at which a child should "be over" grief. We, as human beings, never "get over" our grief, but instead become reconciled to it.) In so doing, bereaved children become capable of establishing new and enriching relationships that give a sense of meaning and purpose to life. Adults who allow and encourage children to move toward their grief, instead of away from it, aid in this reconciliation process.

Among the changes often noted during the child's reconciliation process are

- •a return to stable eating and sleeping pattern,
- •a renewed sense of energy and well-being,
- •a subjective sense of release from the person who has died,
- •increased thinking and judgement making capabilities,
- •the capacity to enjoy life experiences,
- •a recognition of the reality and finality of the death, and
- •the establishment of new and healthy relationships.

Perhaps the most important gain in this reconciliation process for the child is the discovery of the ability to cope successfully with the loss resulting from the death. This coping is achieved only with the assistance of "helping-healing-adults."

Caregiving Behaviors

If we are able to recognize that grief is a complex emotion that varies from child to child, we can be more open and honest in helping young children cope with death and achieve reconciliation. Grief is not something of which a child should be ashamed or try to hide. Only because children are able to give and receive love are they able to grieve and grow. As caregivers, we must model giving and receiving of love as we interact with the child.

In a very real sense, grief is a privilege for both children and adults, in that the capacity for deep feelings exists in a way that lower forms of life are not able to appreciate and experience. Only because we have the capacity for a loving relationship is it possible that we are able to grieve. When children are born into this world, they do not have the choice of feeling or not feeling. The capacity to feel is inevitable. However, as adults, we do have the choice as to how open and honest we will be with our children regarding the full spectrum of feelings and how committed we will be in helping both ourselves and our children in working through these feelings in a healthy, life-giving manner. As caregivers, openness and honesty are essential.

The adult who wants to be a caregiver and help children cope with grief will prepare, plan, and understand grief as an integral part of life and living and will work to reverse the trend toward protecting children from grief. Therefore, if the material shared in this chapter stimulates discussion, raises questions, and increases one's sense of hope, it will have served a most useful purpose.

REFERENCES

Anthony, S. (1971). *The discovery of death in childhood and after.* London: Allan Lan, Penguin.

Bowlby, J. (1973). *Attachment and loss: Separation.* New York: Basic Books.

Engel, G. L. (1971). Sudden and rapid death during psychological stress. *Annals of Internal Medicine, 74,* 771-782.

Kubler-Ross, E. (1969). *On death and dying.* New York: Macmillan.

Melear, J. D. (1973). Children's conceptions of death. *The Journal of Genetic Psychology, 123* (2), 359-360.

Nagy, M. (1948). The child's theories concerning death. *The Journal of Genetic Psychology, 73,* 2-37.

Lindemann, E. (1944). Symptomatology and management of acute grief. *American Journal of Psychiatry, 101,* 141-148.

Parkes, C. M. (1972). *Bereavement: Studies of grief in life.* New York: International Universities Press.

Stillion, J., & Wass, H. (1979). Children and death. In H. Wass (Ed.), *Dying: Facing the facts.* Washington: Hemisphere, 208-235.

Chapter 4

CAREGIVING ASPECTS OF HELPING THE GRIEVING CHILD

(Skills Needed by the "Helping-Healing-Adult")

The child who experiences the death of someone loved does not have the choice between grieving or not grieving, but the adult who has the opportunity to care for the child does have the choice of helping or not helping the child during this vulnerable time. The majority of adults are well aware of a sense of inadequacy when faced with the task of helping children cope with grief. Ironically, through the recognition of this sense of inadequacy and helplessness, parents, teachers, and counselors can become helpful.

The primary philosophy of this book is that

  1. effective communication between adult and child is the essence of helping the child cope with grief;

Caregiving Aspects of Helping the Grieving Child   51

2. more than one tool can be used to help the child express the many thoughts and feelings related to loss; and

3. recognition of the adult helper's own values, thoughts, and feelings related to death and grief is necessary to be capable of helping the grieving child.

Although we as adults learn how to "take-care" of children, unfortunately we often do not learn how to listen, perceive, and respond to them. As a result, an overview of the essential ingredients of helping the bereaved child would seem appropriate. My plan in this chapter is to outline the foundation of skills needed by the "helping-healing-adult" to create healthy responses in children when faced with the experience of loss through death.

PROCESS MODEL FOR HELPING CHILDREN COPE WITH GRIEF

So, what do we as caring adults bring to the grieving child? Hopefully, we bring our sensitivity and warmth, communication of acceptance, and desire to understand (a caring relationship as outlined in Chapter 2), as well as our experience, knowledge, beliefs, and values. Beyond this we bring our personality—our strengths and weaknesses, our way of being in this world, and perhaps most importantly, our genuine affection and regard for children. In other words, we bring ourselves as helpers to the child, caregivers with skills that can aid in the child's growth and development at a critical time in life. In Figure 4.1 is outlined a process model for *Helping Children Cope With Grief*. The process contains three important ingredients to develop the desired outcome: The Helper as a Person *plus* The Caring Relationship *plus* Caregiving Skills *equal* Intended Growth Outcome.

In writing about helping relationships Combs (1967) has used the term "self as instrument" in describing the person's essential helping tool as being oneself—and acting spontaneously in response to the rapidly changing interpersonal demands of the helping relationship. In helping children grow through grief process, one must certainly use the "self as instrument," the first ingredient in the Process Model. The self as instrument helps to create an intimate, unique, and accepting relationship, the

I. *The Helper As A Person* (Self as Instrument)

Related to Life and Death
   Experiences
   Beliefs
   Knowledge
Personality
   Strengths and Weaknesses
   Ways of "Being" in the World
   Genuine Affection and Regard for Children

+

II. *The Caring Relationship*

Sensitivity and Warmth
Communication of Acceptance
Desire to Understand

+

III. *Caregiving Skills*

For Perceiving
For Understanding
For Responding
For Expressing

=

IV. *Intended Growth Outcomes*

For the Child
For the Adult
For Society

Figure 4.1. Process model for helping children cope with grief.

second ingredient between adult and child. In so doing, the helper focuses on the child's perception and needs for the purpose of enhancing the child's adjustment and long-term development. Through use of caregiving skills, the third ingredient, the helper will be able to assist children at this critical time in their lives. However, the helper must recognize that the process often requires a more extensive effort and a greater investment of time on the part of the helper than at any other point during a child's growth and development.

Caregiving skills are divided in this chapter into two major components: (1) communication skills utilized between child and helper and (2) skills for aiding children in expressing grief as shown in Figure 4.2. Three specific communication skills in Figure 4.2 will be the focus of the initial portion of this chapter—attending, listening, and responding with empathetic understanding. The development of skills in these three areas should allow you to create a helping relationship with the grieving child. Following these communication skills will be five skills for aiding children in expressing grief. In addition, included in the content of this chapter are a comprehensive list of techniques used in counseling the bereaved child; an assessment model for the counselor; and specific guidelines for helping the bereaved child.

ATTENDING SKILL

One of the easiest things to do when communicating with children is to focus so much on what they are saying that you are unaware of the nonverbal messages that your body is sending to them. Your attending skill many times determines the child's perception of you and your desire and commitment to help. When a difference exists between what you say and what the child reads nonverbally, the nonverbal behavior is always believed as being true. Children are much more sensitive to visual communication than to the spoken word. Nonverbal language is the first language they learn. The way they are held and touched as infants, expression or tone of voice, and turn of a head all are elements that have meaning to the small child. From these messages they learn how to understand, make sense, and respond to their world. We can easily enhance children's perceptions through an awareness of our nonverbal behavior.

1. Communication Skills Utilized Between Child and Helper

    a. Attending Skill

        Eye Contact
        Posture
        Physical Distance
        Facial Expression
        Gesture
        Setting   Attending Behaviors
        Position
        Voice Tone
        Rate of Speech
        Movement
        Level of Energy

    b. Listening Skill

    c. Responding with Empathy Skill

2. Skills for Aiding Children in Expressing Grief

    a. Paraphrasing Skill

    b. Perception Checking Skill

    c. Questioning Skill

    d. Pacing Skill

    e. Summarizing Skill

Figure 4.2. Caregiving skills.

Attending skill includes the physical behaviors you use while listening to and observing the grieving child. These behaviors—eye contact, posture, physical distance, facial expression, gesture, and the general setting—convey messages to the child that you are attempting to help whenever you are in contact with them. (See Table 4.1). Attending behaviors may be effective or ineffective. Effective attending skill communicates to the child that you are interested and want to be of help. If attending behaviors are ineffective, it is unlikely that a helping relationship will be established between you and the child. My plan is to describe types of attending behaviors and give some suggestions for improving skill in these areas.

Table 4.1

Attending Skill and Related Behaviors:
Effective and Ineffective Use by the Adult Caregiver

EFFECTIVE USE	ATTENDING BEHAVIORS	INEFFECTIVE USE
These behaviors encourage the child's expression of thoughts/feelings because they demonstrate acceptance and respect for the child.	Nonverbal Modes of Communication	Demonstrating any of these things will probably close off or slow down the interaction and relationship between adult and child.
Maintains appropriate gaze, which is not a stare, but does not look away.	EYE CONTACT	Lack of contact, shifts gaze too often or stares.
Leans forward, relaxed, yet attentive.	POSTURE	Stiff and rigid, leaning backward.
Natural distance, three feet, or approximate arms length, touching and comforting when appropriate.	PHYSICAL DISTANCE	Too close, too far away, dependent on child, situation, and relationship.
Reflects the emotional tone of the situation. Communicates a sense of warmth.	FACIAL EXPRESSIONS	Incongruent with the emotional tone of the situation. Expressionless.
Are congruent with content, move slowly and appropriately natural, unobtrusive.	GESTURES	Tense, sudden movements, do not match content, compete for attention with words.

Table 4.1 *(continued)*

Attending Skill and Related Behaviors:
Effective and Ineffective Use by the Adult Caregiver

EFFECTIVE USE	ATTENDING BEHAVIORS	INEFFECTIVE USE
	SETTING	
Draws adult and child together, free from interruptions, pleasant colors, casual vs formal, well-organized.		Physical barriers are present, frequent distractions, dull colors, extremely formal or too casual, disorganized.
	POSITION	
Seated in open position, nothing between self and child, on same eye level.		Barriers like desk or table between self and child, seated in dominant position.
	VOICE TONE	
Voice matches emotional tone of situation, sounds relaxed, has appropriate volume for hearing.		Does not match emotional tone of situation, too loud or too soft, sounds nervous.
	RATE OF SPEECH	
Speaks at natural pace, at times slower than usual.		Too slow or too fast, indicates impatience.
	MOVEMENT	
Toward the child		Away from the child
	LEVEL OF ENERGY	
Maintains alertness throughout interaction with child, natural energy appropriate to the situation.		Has difficulty maintaining concentration, appears sleepy, uninterested, jumpy, pushy, lethargic

Note. Adapted from *The Amity book: Exercises in friendship and helping skills* (p. 53) by R. P. Walters, 1975. Copyright 1975 by Richard P. Walters.

No specific rules exist to follow when using the attending skill. However, some general principles will help you use behaviors that are effective and avoid those that are ineffective. Guidelines for the attending skill and related behaviors will allow you to express your own uniqueness as a helping person when you are involved with a child at this critical time. The balance of this section contains suggested guidelines for six of the eleven behaviors related to the attending skill.

Eye Contact

Perhaps the most effective way of making contact with children is through the use of your *eyes*. Eyes are one of the key modes of nonverbal communication and a helpful way of communicating your concern and interest. While a fixed stare would be inappropriate, it is quite appropriate to look at the child you are helping both while talking and during time of silence. A good rule of thumb is that eye contact should be maintained at least half of the time during your interaction with the child.

Posture

A second component of attending skill is *posture*. Each moment of every day we all communicate much by how we stand, sit, and walk. Take a moment to become aware of your own posture and what is communicated to someone entering the room. When you are involved in a helping relationship with bereaved children, make sure that your posture communicates an interest and readiness to assist them. It is also helpful to communicate a sense of relaxation with your posture as it can have an important calming effect on the child you are aiding. If you are tense, you will take the focus away from the child and put it on yourself. Posture also communicates something about your energy level. It is easy to lean against the door or a wall as you interact, yet to many children this will mean that you are not "with them" because of your energy level.

Physical Distance

A third component of attending is *physical distance* between you and the child. At times it is quite appropriate to move in very close as you reach out to comfort. Of course, this also depends on the strength of your relationship with the child. Use the reaction of the child as a guide. If the child pulls away from you, take that as an indication that you are too close, or that your relationship is not strong enough to be that close.

Facial Expression

A fourth component of attending is your *facial expression.* The expression on your face should match as closely as possible what is occurring around you. Your facial expression can easily communicate a sense of warmth as well as a message that "I am with you, I understand, and I want to help." You may find that you communicate something different with your facial expression than you intend. After all, facial expression is something that is most difficult to observe unless you look in a mirror. You might want to ask your family, friends, and the children around you how they perceive your different facial expressions.

Gesture

A fifth component of attending is *gesture.* You communicate much with your body movements. The gestures you make should be natural and not interfere with your intended communication. If you move quickly or have mannerisms that are distracting, you will take much away from your ability to help the child. Ask yourself if messages you give with your gestures are those you intend to communicate.

Setting

A sixth attending element is the *setting.* Of course, there are times when you have little if any control over the setting. Your initial contact with the child may be in the home, the hospital, or the school. However, when possible, take advantage of the opportunity to create a setting that is most conducive to effective helping. If you are a counselor, your office or playroom should be a place that affords the child your undivided attention. Interruptions and distractions should be eliminated as much as possible. Furniture and toys can be arranged in a way that draws people together as opposed to spacing them apart. Pleasant colors can be used for both the furniture and the walls. Desks or tables only serve to hinder the communication process between adult and child. By getting out from behind your desk, you are able to involve yourself with the child and better communicate your openness.

Highlighting Attending Skill

In Table 4.1 are listed eleven behaviors related to the attending skill. In general terms, these behaviors may be either effective or ineffective. Caregiving adults who make use of effective attending behaviors can anticipate a number of important benefits:

Caregiving Aspects of Helping the Grieving Child   59

1. Positive attending behaviors by you will give permission to the child you are helping to feel his/her true feelings because you are giving fully of your own time, energy, and attention. This helps build a healing relationship.

2. Your positive attending behaviors will communicate to the child that you are trying to understand. You are listening to the child, which makes him/her aware of your concern.

3. Your positive attending behaviors will help you focus on the child and respond in a helpful manner.

Ineffective attending behaviors tend to close off conversation or prohibit a helping relationship from being established between adult and child. If you find yourself unable to attend effectively over a period of time, you will most likely notice some changes in the child's behavior. The child may become passive and find it difficult to share the hurt with you in a mutual relationship. The result may be that you find yourself moving into a question/answer pattern with the child in an attempt to drag out his/her thoughts and feelings. On the other hand, the child may become upset, impatient, and angry because you do not appear interested or concerned. These are signs that your attending skill is lacking at that time and that the child is not satisfied with the level of attention you are offering.

ASSESSING YOUR OWN NONVERBAL ATTENDING BEHAVIORS

Assessing one's own nonverbal attending behaviors often is difficult. However through studying Table 4.1 it is possible to increase your awareness of your behavior. Through being consciously aware of how you are coming across in your interaction with the grieving child, you can enhance the impact you are having. Most adults de-emphasize the importance of the attending skill in communication with children. But when you realize that the majority of effective communication with a child is nonverbal, then the importance of attending skill development is evident.

Activity 4.1
ATTENDING SKILL

Participating in the following activity will enable you to enhance your attending skill. Find a child with whom you can engage in a discussion about any topic of interest for approximately five minutes. Using the items outlined in Table 4.1 become aware of your attending behaviors. Ask another adult to observe your interaction with the child and to rate you using the Rating Scale for Attending Skill (Table 4.2). Upon completion of your five-minute interaction with the child ask the observer-rater to comment on your attending behaviors, focusing on both positive and negative aspects of your nonverbal communication. Practice this activity with different children until you feel you have reached an effective level of attending behavior toward children.

Notes:

Table 4.2

Rating Scale for Attending Skill

The categories High, Medium, and Low will be used to identify the quality of the helping adult's attending behavior. The following statements are definitions of high, medium, and low levels of attending behavior.

High (H) Response—Helping adult looked at child; looked interested, relaxed, yet attentive; emotional tone of voice appropriate to situation; and maintained appropriate eye contact. Each behavior was present all of the time.

Medium (M) Response—Helping adult demonstrated high attending behaviors at least part of the time.

Low (L) Response—Helping adult did not exhibit high attending behavior and seldom, if ever, looked at the child.

Rating (Check One) L M H	Attending Behavior	Comments
__ __ __	Eye Contact	_____ _____
__ __ __	Posture	_____ _____
__ __ __	Physical Distance	_____ _____
__ __ __	Facial Expression	_____ _____
__ __ __	Gestures	_____ _____
__ __ __	Setting	_____ _____

Table 4.2 *(continued)*

Rating Scale for Attending Skill

Rating (Check One) L M H	Attending Behavior	Comments
___ ___ ___	Position	
___ ___ ___	Voice Tone	
___ ___ ___	Rate of Speech	
___ ___ ___	Movement	
___ ___ ___	Level of Energy	

INTERPRETING THE CHILD'S NONVERBAL BEHAVIORS

Many adults believe that nonverbal communication with children involves eye contact, facial expression, gestures, and not much more. It is true that nonverbal communication is all those things, but it is more—much more. Every aspect of what children observe in us and what we observe in children is nonverbal—except for the words used. Therefore, areas like tone of voice, rate of speech, and physical distance are areas of which we can be aware when interacting with grieving children. These cues, in addition to words used, give us clues about the children we wish to help.

The nonverbal world of children is very complex, and it is unfair and many times inaccurate to form opinions of children based upon a single nonverbal behavior. However, you can form an idea based on a small amount of nonverbal evidence and then either confirm or deny the notion based upon additional verbal and nonverbal information.

Children do not always ask for help in words. A grieving child, for example, often cannot verbally state clearly what is wanted, but expressions and body tension may be crying out, "Please help me!" Our inferences from reading such behavior could be wrong, but the only way caring adults will know is to respond, and then be alert to the child's reaction.

One of the most effective ways to use knowledge of a child's nonverbal behavior is to respond to it verbally.

Illustration: Seven-year-old David was discovered by his teacher hiding in the classroom closet only two weeks after the sudden and unexpected death of his father. His teacher responded to his nonverbal behavior by commenting, "David, you look like you are pretty scared right now?" David, feeling understood by his teacher stated tearfully, "Yes, I'm scared. I'm afraid my Mommy will die and leave me too." In this example, David's teacher responded in a way that allowed a dialogue to begin between adult and child—a vital component to the establishment of a healing relationship.

There are many advantages to responding to the grieving child's nonverbal behavior as illustrated previously. Some of the more important reasons are as follows:

    1. The responding behavior creates a feeling on the part of the child that "the adult understands me."
    2. It helps establish rapport with the child.
    3. The child will be more at ease because of the rapport.
    4. You help the child move toward their grief instead of away from it.

A frequent question I am asked is, "What if I say something about a child's nonverbal message, and I am wrong in reading the behavior?" This is a good question because it is true that if you continue to "miss" in responding to nonverbal behavior, you will lose credibility in the eyes of the child. But, surprisingly, what happens if you miss only occasionally is that *the child will help you out.* What is communicated is "you are trying to understand me and that is good."

Illustration: Eleven-year-old Frank's Father died two months ago. In talking with a caregiving adult Frank said, "I just don't know what to do." The caregiver responded, "Frank, I'm in-

*terested in you and want to help. Right now you sound scared."
Frank responded, "No, I'm not scared, I'm mad. I'm mad
because my daddy died." What is not usually said, but
understood by the child is "I like your being concerned about
me." So when you miss once in a while, the intent of your
message (i.e., your concern) is still communicated to the child.*

The fact that you might occasionally miss, then, should not
discourage you from "tuning into" the nonverbal domain of the child.
This is a skill, and as a skill, your batting average will improve with practice, with the end result being good feelings between you and the child
you are helping.

One common occurrence is when the child says one thing and you
read something else in the nonverbal behavior. This is a problem that requires having some skill in order to respond appropriately. A good rule
of thumb is that the nonverbal is usually true, but until the relationship is
strong you acknowledge only the verbal.

*Illustration: Twelve-year-old Kelly says, "I'm just not going to
be sad about Grandpa's death" and yet you see definite signs of
sadness and grief. You might respond by saying, "Well, I'll be
here to talk if you decide you want to." Once rapport is
established, to the same statement you might say, "Kelly, you
say you're not going to be sad, but I can tell you have some pretty strong feelings about your Grandpa's death. Do you think
maybe you and I can talk about your Grandpa?" It should be
obvious why the second response, actually a type of confronta-
tion, would be inappropriate if the relationship was not strong.*

To summarize, the strength of the relationship determines whether
or not the discrepancy between verbal and nonverbal communication
should be brought out.

The previous information helps you in the process of awareness and
observations of grieving children. However, it is important to remember
that nonverbal behaviors must always be judged in context and their
meaning considered tentative. Use your perception of nonverbal
behaviors as clues to possible underlying thoughts and feelings rather
than as proof that they exist. For example, tears on the part of the grieving child may come from confusion, anger, guilt, or relief. Silence may
occur in your interaction with the child out of a sense of being overwhelmed, lack of understanding, need for a quiet moment, or a need to

relate to others in communicative silence. Making and acting on quick interpretations are very likely to get you into trouble, so always set the child's nonverbal behavior in context.

Activity 4.2
FOCUSING ON THE NONVERBAL
COMMUNICATION OF CHILDREN

Participating in the following activity will enable you to enhance your understanding of children's nonverbal communication. Find a child whom you can engage in a discussion about any topic of interest for approximately five minutes. Observe the nonverbal communication used by the child during your interaction.

List the nonverbal behaviors that seem to enhance your understanding of the child.

List other nonverbal behaviors that seem to cause your dialogue with the child to move ahead and that might indicate that the child is accepting you as a caring person who is interested.

Notes:

LISTENING: A VITAL INGREDIENT TO HELPING THE GRIEVING CHILD
(Listening Skill)

The development of a "helping-healing-relationship" requires the adult to attend to and concentrate as completely as possible on what is going on in the "here and now" for the grieving child. Being able to understand what the child's world is like requires the ability to listen intently and purposefully. Listening to the child is an effective way of putting care into action. Listening may appear to be a passive process, but in reality it is an active process that is hard work. It involves a comprehensive type of perceptiveness that Reik (1948) has described as "listening with the third ear."

Listening requires hearing not only the content of what the child is saying but also hearing the content of that which is only being hinted. The child may need help in terms of being able to put thoughts and feelings into words. While you will certainly want to listen with your ears and see through your eyes, you also will want to hear and respond with your heart.

Listening also requires sharing responsibility for communication as only part of the responsibility rests with the child. As you increasingly learn to listen for the purpose of better understanding, there will undoubtedly be times when you do not understand what the child is attempting to communicate. Expecting differently from yourself would be unrealistic. Take your time and patiently listen to the child. If you expect yourself to comprehend instantly the total meaning of the child's communication and to heal immediately the child's grief, chances are that you will do a poor job of listening. If you find yourself being impatient in your effort to understand, you may unknowingly be treating the aftermath of the death in the child's life as an event rather than a process.

Another indicator that you may be trying to move the child too quickly through experience with grief is finding yourself talking at the child instead of listening. Unfortunately, there are times when out of our sense of urgency to help the child we become more concerned with "preaching" to the child than with listening and responding. Hopefully, we can recognize that we do not have to attempt to be all-wise and all-knowing to our children. The process of responding in a listening way is a prerequisite to responding with an empathetic orientation.

As you develop the ability to listen to the child with understanding, you also may discover you are better able to understand yourself. The positive consequence of this phenomenon is that you will be able to listen to the child and yourself at the same time. You will be able to hear and respond at an appropriate level of understanding. To be capable of listening to yourself as well as the child is testimony to the fact that both you and the child are involved in the relationship. After all, there is no relationship without a minimum of two people.

You may ask yourself "Well, just what is it that I should attempt to understand in the grieving child's communication with me?" While certainly no one answer is feasible to this question, perhaps it will be helpful to outline some areas where it is important to listen for the purpose of better understanding the child. Among the questions I consider are the following:

1. What is the "meaning" of this death from the child's perspective; how did the child view his/her relationship with the person who died?

2. From whom does the child feel a sense of support at this time? Does the child perceive self as being in a loving, trusting environment?

3. How does the child think and feel about self right now; how might this be different than prior to the experience of death?

4. How does the child think and feel about others, particularly about significant others? Does the child see significant others as being rendered helpless by their grief? Does the child feel abandoned by family members?

5. How does the child view others' thinking and feeling, about him/her, particularly significant others?

6. What does the child want and need in this relationship? How am I perceived as caregiver?

7. What rules exist within the child related to the expression of thoughts and feelings? What messages have been received related to the expression of painful feelings?

8. What coping mechanisms are used?

9. As I search for understanding, how do I feel in this relationship?

Obviously, this list is not all inclusive and is only intended as an initial guide. In the final analysis, purposeful listening can only take place when the child is not threatened by it. Allowing yourself to become comfortable in the listening-helping role will make it possible for the child to become more comfortable with self and with you. The child will feel accepted and return the feeling. You may discover that the reason the child feels accepted by you is because you have accepted yourself in this helping role.

Activity 4.3
LISTENING FOR UNDERSTANDING

The following activity will enable you to enhance your listening for understanding skills. Find a child whom you can engage in a discussion about any topic of interest for approximately five minutes. During the discussion, state in your own words what the child has said and also communicate in your own words feelings expressed. If the child conveys an acceptance of your perceptions, a good chance exists that you have listened and understood.

How was the acceptance communicated?

How do you feel about what happened during the discussion?

Notes:

THE IMPORTANCE OF
EMPATHETIC UNDERSTANDING
(Responding with Empathy Skill)

Perhaps the most essential helping skill is the ability to communicate accurately empathy to the grieving child. The first step in communicating empathy involves the adult's ability to recognize and understand inner experiences and feelings of the child as the child experiences them. This means the adult must develop the capacity to project oneself into the child's world, to view the situation through the child's eyes—to understand the meaning of his/her experience, instead of imposing meaning on that experience from the outside.

To be empathetic does not mean that you experience the same emotion as the child—this would be sympathy. To attempt to experience the same emotions as the child would be overinvolvment, and fortunately it is not necessary to experience personally the child's feelings to be helpful. Whereas sympathy involves the expression of compassion and care for the child, empathy does not involve the direct expression of one's own feelings, but instead focuses on the feelings expressed by the child, and as a result communicates an understanding of these feelings.

Empathy involves expansion of oneself to include the child—the flexibility to expand one's boundary. It is not identifying or losing oneself, but merging with the child's experiences. To achieve a sense of merging with the child once again requires a here-and-now awareness of the thinking and feeling world of the child. To become capable of this awareness means being open not only to the content of what the child says, but also to the nonverbal cues such as facial expression, tone of voice, gesture, and posture that reinforce or at times contradict the verbal messages.

While empathetic understanding is difficult in and of itself, it is not enough. The adult also must be able to communicate accurately this sense of understanding to the child. In other words, understanding alone is not enough; the adult also must accurately convey that understanding. The ability to let children know that you understand their feelings helps them feel secure, trusting, warm, and affirmed. This ability is the essence of a "helping-healing" relationship.

In Table 4.3 are listed some words of feelings experienced by children. These feelings are ones an empathetic adult can recognize and

Table 4.3

Partial List of Positive and Negative Feeling Words

POSITIVE		NEGATIVE	
alert	happy	afraid	guilty
alive	hopeful	angry	hateful
amazed	interested	annoyed	helpless
busy	involved	anxious	hurt
calm	joyful	bad	lonely
comfortable	loving	bitter	mad
concerned	peaceful	bored	mean
confident	proud	concerned	nervous
curious	quiet	confused	sad
eager	relieved	depressed	scared
elated	secure	disappointed	sorry
excited	surprised	discouraged	unhappy
friendly	trusting	disliked	upset
glad	warm	embarrassed	worried
good		frightened	

Note. Included in this table is a partial list of words of feelings experienced by children to which an empathetic adult should be able to respond.

then make a response. By responding empathetically you help the child to accept these feelings in him/herself and to understand the importance of those feelings. Where necessary, and often it is, you can help the child express more completely those feelings and in doing so help the child work through those feelings.

At times, parents, teachers, and counselors shy away from acknowledging feelings in the grieving child such as anger, sadness, fear, or guilt. A common reason given for not acknowledging these feelings in the child is the thought that in discussing such feelings one would only make the child feel worse. However, my experience suggests that such reasoning is more often related to the adult's uneasiness in responding at an emotional level than to the thought that the child will be hurt by this experience. Instead, recognizing and encouraging the child to talk about

Caregiving Aspects of Helping the Grieving Child   71

such feelings allows the child to view the adult as someone capable of exploring such scary feelings. My belief is that we should never avoid what a grieving child is feeling because we are afraid he/she cannot take it. Obviously the child is already taking it. The question is *"Will the child experience these feelings in isolation or in the comfort of loving adults?"* To allow grieving children to live alone during their time of grief is mismanagement of a helping opportunity.

What is the effect on the grieving child when you respond to him/her with empathy? First of all, empathetic communication allows for the establishment of a relationship with the child. The child who feels empathetically understood is more likely to share personal thoughts and feelings. The child also will recognize that you are listening and understanding what is wished for you to understand. Before responding to the child's feelings, caregivers must realize that recognizing their own feelings is an important first step toward making healthy contact with the child.

Illustration: Twelve-year-old Bobby whose Grandfather had died recently began having temper tantrums in class at school and failed to complete his work. None of his teacher's attempts to reach him had been successful. Bobby's teacher began to realize her own sense of frustration and anger that occurred when she wanted to relate to Bobby and was unable to do so. In consultation, the teacher was able to realize that she had been attempting to make contact with Bobby by asking a number of "why" questions. "Why don't you want to do your work?" "Why won't you talk to me?" "Why are you being so difficult?" By becoming aware of how unproductive this kind of approach was, the teacher was able to shift to responses more descriptive of his behavior (without blame) and intended to produce more interaction and less guilt. In doing so the teacher expressed her own feelings while at the same time sharing her awareness that Bobby's change in behavior could have been, and probably was, related to his Grandfather's recent death.

"Bobby, I want to understand what you are feeling. When I can't, I feel angry and frustrated at both myself and you. I know your Grandpa just died and that you miss him very much. I hope that you and I can talk about what you're feeling. I guess I need you to help me help you."

Activity 4.4
SKILL DEVELOPMENT IN RESPONDING
WITH EMPATHY

To enable you to enhance your ability to respond with empathy the following activity is provided for your participation. The activity is divided into two parts. The first part is ten messages that will provide you with practice in identifying feelings of grieving children. Below each statement, list the words that best describe feelings of the child. To be helpful to the child you must be accurate not only in perceiving feelings, but also in responding to them as well. To develop this skill you will need to practice.

Statements 11 through 20 will provide you an opportunity to write responses to Statements 1 through 10 in response form rather than just words. The intent is to reflect to the child the content and the feelings of what he/she has said. Read the child's message in an effort to perceive any and all feelings invested in it. Fill in the practice response first, and then in your own way complete the natural response. Recognize that at first your response will tend to sound mechanical and rehearsed, but that as time passes your responses will become more spontaneous. You may wish to refer to Table 4.3 to help you in describing the child's feelings.

1. "At times, I think I should have known that something was wrong with Dad and made him go to the doctor. But I didn't."

Feelings Expressed:

2. "All my friends at school don't say a word to me about my Mom since she died. At times I need someone to talk to about her, but there is no one."

Feelings Expressed:

Caregiving Aspects of Helping the Grieving Child   73

3. "I don't know why the doctors didn't do something sooner. It was like they didn't even care about Grandpa because he was old. I would really like to tell them what I think of them."

Feelings Expressed:

4. "I miss Mom so much. I could always tell her anything and she seemed to know just what to say."

Feelings Expressed:

5. "I just don't feel like doing anything. Everybody tries to make me be happy right now, but I'm not. Why don't they just leave me alone?"

Feelings Expressed:

6. "I miss Grandpa, but he was sick for so long and he was having lots of pain. Maybe I shouldn't feel this way, but I'm glad he doesn't hurt anymore."

Feelings Expressed:

7. "My friends still have Dads and I don't. I just don't think it's fair."

Feelings Expressed:

8. "My teacher lets me talk about my feelings. She even set up a special time when I could talk to her about Mom. I feel like she really cares about me."

Feelings Expressed:

9. "Since my Dad died, I keep thinking something is going to happen to my Mom. It's really hard for me to leave Mom alone right now. She probably thinks I'm a big baby."

Feelings Expressed:

10. "Right after Mom died all of my friends really seemed to care about me, but now they don't. I don't think anybody cares about me."

Feelings Expressed:

11. (Using Statement #1) Practice Response:
You feel   because

Natural Response:

12. (Using Statement #2) Practice Response:
You feel   because

Natural Response:

13. (Using Statement #3) Practice Response:
You feel   because

Natural Response:

14. (Using Statement #4) Practice Response:
You feel   because

Natural Response:

Caregiving Aspects of Helping the Grieving Child   75

15. (Using Statement #5) Practice Response:
You feel   because
Natural Response:

16. (Using Statement #6) Practice Response:
You feel   because

Natural Response:

17. (Using Statement #7) Practice Response:
You feel   because

Natural Response:

18. (Using Statement #8) Practice Response:
You feel   because

Natural Response:

19. (Using Statement #9) Practice Response:
You feel   because

Natural Response:

20. (Using Statement #10) Practice Response:)
You feel   because

Natural Response:

Notes:

SKILLS FOR AIDING CHILDREN
IN EXPRESSING GRIEF

At this point in your reading you have begun to recognize the belief that a warm, trusting relationship between adult and child underlies any strategy or approach to the helping process and, as a result, is a major condition for any effective helping to take place. Developing this helping-healing relationship is a time-consuming process; however, a committed adult can guide this development so that the relationship can aid the child within a short period of time.

Inherent in the relationship are those skills based upon the responsive listening format which focus on hearing verbal and observing nonverbal messages of the child and on responding to those messages both verbally and nonverbally. You must continually ask yourself: "What is this child really trying to say to me?" Then use skills that will aid the child in expressing grief. In this section five skills are discussed that you can use to aid the child. The five skills are as follows:

1. paraphrasing skill,
2. perception-checking skill,
3. questioning skill,
4. pacing skill, and
5. summarizing skill.

The information supplied regarding these helping skills is only intended as an introductory overview. To assist yourself in a more comprehensive grasp of these and other skills you should refer to texts listed under Suggestions For Further Study at the end of this chapter.

Paraphrasing Skill

1. What the skill is

•restating the child's basic message in similar and most often fewer words.
•stating in your own words what the child has said.
•extracting the essence of what the child has said.

2. Purposes for using this skill

 •testing your understanding of what the child has said.
 •communicates to the child that you are attempting to understand what you're told. You are actively listening, making the child aware of your concern.

3. Illustrations of the use of paraphrasing

 To help in this process ask yourself: "What is this child trying to communicate to me?"

 Illustration A. Child: "My teacher really seems to know when I'm feeling sad about my Mom's death. She lets me know its okay to talk with her about my feelings."

 Helping Adult: "You really like your teacher's concern for you."

 Child: "Yes, she really cares about me..."

 Illustration B. Child: "When Grandpa was in the hospital the nurses would let me visit as long as I wanted. They helped me understand what they were doing to try to help him."

 Helping Adult: "It sounds like those nurses were a big help to you and your Grandpa."

 Child: "They sure were..."

4. Outcomes expected by the helping adult

 •the child experiences a feeling of being understood and accepted.

 •the child has a clearer perception of what was said.

 •the child has a sense of direction in diaiogue with you.

 •the child is enouraged to continue to express thoughts and feelings to you.

Perception-Checking Skill

1. What the skill is

 •asking the child to confirm your perceptions of what he/she has said.

•asking the child for feedback regarding the accuracy of your response.
•checking with the child instead of simply assuming that understanding is taking place.

2. Purposes for using the skill

•allows you to test your understanding of what the child has said.
•allows you an excellent method of giving and receiving feedback on the accuracy of your communication with the child.

3. Illustrations of the use of perception checking

Illustration A. Helping Adult: "Sounds as if you're really scared that something might happen to your Mom and that no one would be left to take care of you. Is that right?"

Illustration B. Helping Adult: "I want to be sure I know what you are saying. You said that nobody talks to you about your Grandpa and that you wish they would?"

Illustration C. Helping Adult: "You would like to talk with your Mom about your Dad, but you are afraid it will make her cry— Right?"

4. Outcomes expected by the helping adult

•helps the child experience a feeling of being understood and accepted.
•clarifies communications quickly.
•misperceptions are corrected before they become misunderstandings.
•encourages the child to continue to express thoughts and feelings.

Questioning Skill

Adults often are tempted to begin a dialogue with a child by asking questions and getting answers, asking more questions and getting more answers. If you find yourself asking questions, you may find that you are setting up a pattern which neither you nor the child will be able to break easily. By initiating this pattern you will be communicating to the grieving child that it is up to you to ask the questions and it is up to the child to answer. In effect, what happens is that the child becomes an object; an object that answers when asked and otherwise keeps quiet. In starting a question-answer pattern you are telling the child as plainly as if you said it in words that you are the authority, the one in charge, and that only you know what is important or relevant.

1. What the skill is

> •a way of gaining information from the child and increasing your depth of understanding.

2. Purposes for using the skill

> •to gain information so that you can assist the child in coping with grief.
> •to increase understanding for both you and the child.

Open-ended Vs. Closed-ended Questions. A distinction must be made between asking the child permissive (open) questions rather than pointed (closed) questions. The permissive question is broad and encourages the child to talk freely; the pointed question is narrow in focus and may inadvertently put answers in the child's mouth. The permissive question communicates a willingness to assist the child in exploration; the pointed question limits response to a specific answer. The permissive question encourages the child to express thoughts and feelings; the pointed question often requests the facts only. And, perhaps most importantly, permissive questions help to establish rapport and openness with the child; pointed questions often create a distance in the interpersonal relationship.

3. Illustrations of the use of questioning

Open-ended Vs. Closed-ended Questions. The following illustrations contain a comparison of permissive (open-ended) questions and pointed (closed-ended) questions. In each illustration the content of the question is approximately the same; however, the structure (i.e., permissive vs. pointed) will result in totally different responses on the part of the child.

> *Illustration A.*
> *Pointed: "Do you want to go to the funeral?"*
>
> *Permissive: "What do you think about going to the funeral?"*

Illustration B.
Pointed: "Do you remember some good times with your Dad?"

Permissive: "What are some of the times you remember best with your Dad?"

4. Outcomes expected by the helping adult

You should be able to:
- help the child become more open to you.
- get information without seeming to demand it.
- create a relationship with permissive questioning that allows you to help the child.
- help maintain the dialogue.
- gain an increased understanding for both yourself and the child.

Pacing Skill

Also important is trying to adjust your pace to that of the child. To proceed too slowly often communicates a lack of interest or understanding. To proceed too rapidly is to risk the possibilities of discussing too lightly important items the child may need to explore, of confusing the child, and that by suggesting different ways indicating that you are really not interested in what is being said. You also must accept the pace of the child in the sense of not pushing to reveal anymore than the child is ready to reveal at any one time. Of course, you must first establish a relationship with the child before exploring areas of difficulty for the child.

Summarizing Skill

1. What the skill is

- reviewing with the child the major thoughts and feelings expressed at points of transition in your dialogue or at the end of your dialogue.

2. Purposes for using the skill

- to increase understanding for both you and the child.
- to aid in transition from one topic area to another.

Caregiving Aspects of Helping the Grieving Child   81

•to give the child a sense of progress in the exploration of thoughts and feelings.

3. Illustrations of the use of summarizing

   Illustration A. "Let's go over what you and I have talked about today . . . ."

   Illustration B. "What you and I have been saying is . . . ."

4. Outcome expected by the helping adult

   The adult can expect that the child will

   •be reassured that you have heard what has been said.
   •be encouraged to develop a different way of viewing thoughts and feelings.
   •have an increased understanding and awareness of concerns he/she might have.
   •have cleared up any confusion that might have occurred.

THE LOSS INVENTORY

Use of the *Loss Inventory for Kids* (reproduced in Table 4.4) enables the helping adult to determine the cumulative effect loss events may have on a child. The inventory considers many situations, including death of a significant person and the relative time of the event in order to calculate the cumulative effect.

Completing the *Loss Inventory for Kids* can be beneficial for a grieving child. Reading and completing the inventory can help the child to understand some possible causes for his/her feelings in addition to feelings directly related to an obvious loss. The helping adult can use skills developed in this chapter to further the child's understanding and reconciliation of the loss.

Table 4.4

Loss Inventory for Kids

Directions

1. Read the loss listed on the next page.

2. When you have completed that loss, place an "x" in the appropriate "time factor" box.

3. When you have completed the entire inventory of losses, tally each loss as follows: *Multiply "impact factor" by "time factor" and enter the answer in the far right column. Add "total" column vertically for your total score.*

4. See score impact information at the end of this inventory.

LOSS INVENTORY FOR KIDS	IMPACT FACTOR	TIME FACTOR			IMPACT "X" TIME FACTOR
		0 - 6 months	6 mos. - 1 year	1 year - 4 years	
		X 5	X 3	X 1	
Death of parent	10				
Death of brother/sister	10				
Divorce of parents	10				
Extended separation of parents (no divorce)	10				
Diagnosed terminal illness self/parent/sibling	10				
Death of close relative	9				
Moving to new city	9				
Major personal injury or illness (loss of limb, etc.)	9				
Abortion	9				
Rape	9				
Marriage/remarriage of parent	8				
Unplanned job loss—self/parent (fired, layed off)	8				
Retirement—parent	8				
				Sub-total	

Caregiving Aspects of Helping the Grieving Child   83

Table 4.4 *(continued)*

LOSS INVENTORY FOR KIDS	IMPACT FACTOR	TIME FACTOR 0 - 6 months X 5	TIME FACTOR 6 mos. - 1 year X 3	TIME FACTOR 1 year - 4 years X 1	IMPACT "X" TIME FACTOR
Unwanted pregnancy	8				
Changing to new school	8				
Major change in a family member (health, behavior)	8				
Moved or kicked out of home before age 18	8				
Permanent suspension from school	8				
Gaining new family member (birth, adoption, relative)	7				
Change in financial status of family (much better/worse)	7				
Love relationship breakup	7				
Death of a friend	7				
Diagnosed ID	6				
Loss of harmony (conflicts) with parents, teachers, friends	6				
Brother/sister leaving home (marriage, college, run-away)	6				
Mother beginning work or going back to school	6				
Class/teacher/schedule change	5				
Sporadic school attendance	5				
Moving within city	5				
Beginning/end of school	5				
Taking new job after school	5				
Temporary separations within family (military, business)	4				
Change in physical appearance (pimples, glasses, etc.)	4				
Violations of the law (drugs, speeding)	4				
Trouble in school (teacher/principal)	4				
Sub-total					

Table 4.4 *(continued)*

LOSS INVENTORY FOR KIDS	IMPACT FACTOR	TIME FACTOR			IMPACT "X" TIME FACTOR
		0 - 6 months	6 mos. - 1 year	1 year - 4 years	
		X 5	X 3	X 1	
Change in living conditions (sharing a room, remodelling)	3				
Christmas/Easter/Vacations	3				
Daily success loss (A to B on paper, didn't make team)	3				
Argument with friend	3				
				Sub-total this page	
				Sub-total 1st page	
				Sub-total 2nd page	
				Composite score	

Impact

Under 150: probably have not faced major losses within the last year. It is not that your life is without loss; however, you should have adjusted to the losses that have occurred.

150-300: you are experiencing an average amount of loss in your life. More than likely you have experienced no or very few major losses within the last year. The losses you experienced did cause a change in your life and warranted some adjustment from you. However, there should not have been great confusion/pain with this adjustment.

300-400: may have experienced several high level losses in the last four years, or one major loss in the last year. The losses may have caused a degree of confusion/pain and readjustment may have been difficult and prolonged.

400 and up: probably have experienced multiple high level losses within the last year. These losses more than likely have affected you physically and emotionally. Adjusting to the losses has been painful and confusing, and there have been major interuptions that you have had to deal with.

Note. From *Perspectives on Loss: A Manual for Educators,* (pp. 16-17) by B. A. Babensee & J. R. Pequette, 1982, P.O. Box 1352 Evergreen, CO: Copyright 1982 by B. A. Babensee & J. R. Pequette. Reprinted by permission.

Caregiving Aspects of Helping the Grieving Child   85

FOCUS ON THE COUNSELOR
Components and Techniques Used
in Counseling the Bereaved Child

Those of you who work as child counselors are aware that the components and techniques of helping children vary from one counselor to another. Because no one counseling technique is appropriate for all bereaved children, additional counseling techniques have naturally evolved. Research and experimentation have led to new methods of helping children and to an identification of which techniques are most appropriate when using a specific theoretical base with a child. As a result, the counseling profession has developed to the point that you as a counselor can select techniques according to your own philosophical base and according to the needs of the child. In recognizing your own limitations in using a wide range of techniques, this knowledge will enable you to refer certain children, seek consultation when working with some children, request a team-approach to work with certain children, or limit your practice to children within your own range of competency (Hollis, 1980, p. 80).

In Table 4.5 are listed techniques of counseling for use with the bereaved child. The list is not all inclusive but does represent a variety of techniques. Suggestions are that you first examine the techniques listed in Table 4.5. Then technique by technique decide the extent to which you would be competent to use each. Indicate the extent of use by checking the appropriate letter. If you do not know the technique or how it might be used to help the bereaved child, then check under the "X" as an indication that the technique is unknown. Space is provided at the end of the list for you to add other techniques that you use.

No one person probably would be skilled in all techniques listed nor does he/she need to feel the necessity to be competent in all. To know and use effectively some 8 to 15 techniques would be sufficient. To know which ones you can use and which ones you cannot use competently is the important aspect. If a certain technique is needed with a given child, you may ask someone to assist you or have the person who is competent in that technique work with the child instead of or in conjunction with you.

Should you so choose, your second task is to become more knowledgeable of the techniques which you do not know—the ones marked with "X". As you gain knowledge relating to each technique, you can decide whether or not you will use it and with which particular children and under what conditions.

Techniques of Counseling for Use with Bereaved Children

	EXTENT OF USE OF TECHNIQUE						EXTENT OF USE OF TECHNIQUE			
Technique Unknown	None	Minimal	Average	Extensive	TECHNIQUE	Technique Unknown	None	Minimal	Average	Extensive	TECHNIQUE
X	N	M	A	E	TECHNIQUE	X	N	M	A	E	TECHNIQUE
—	—	—	—	—	acceptance	—	—	—	—	—	play therapy
—	—	—	—	—	active listening	—	—	—	—	—	positive reinforcement
—	—	—	—	—	art therapy	—	—	—	—	—	probing questioning
—	—	—	—	—	attending	—	—	—	—	—	reassurance
—	—	—	—	—	audio recorded models	—	—	—	—	—	recollection of memories
—	—	—	—	—	bibliotherapy	—	—	—	—	—	re-education
—	—	—	—	—	catharsis	—	—	—	—	—	reflection
—	—	—	—	—	clarifying	—	—	—	—	—	regression
—	—	—	—	—	confrontation	—	—	—	—	—	reinforcement
—	—	—	—	—	contractual agreements	—	—	—	—	—	restatement of content
—	—	—	—	—	congruence	—	—	—	—	—	self-disclosure
—	—	—	—	—	decision making	—	—	—	—	—	self-modeling
—	—	—	—	—	desensitization	—	—	—	—	—	silence
—	—	—	—	—	dream interpretation	—	—	—	—	—	summarization
—	—	—	—	—	education	—	—	—	—	—	supporting
—	—	—	—	—	empathy	—	—	—	—	—	tell a story
—	—	—	—	—	encouragement	—	—	—	—	—	termination
—	—	—	—	—	environment manipulation	—	—	—	—	—	value clarification
—	—	—	—	—	explaining	—	—	—	—	—	warmth
—	—	—	—	—	family group counseling						
—	—	—	—	—	fantasizing						Add Your Own Techniques
—	—	—	—	—	feedback						
—	—	—	—	—	first memory	—	—	—	—	—	_____
—	—	—	—	—	group play	—	—	—	—	—	_____
—	—	—	—	—	interpretation	—	—	—	—	—	_____
—	—	—	—	—	journal keeping	—	—	—	—	—	_____
—	—	—	—	—	leading modeling	—	—	—	—	—	_____
—	—	—	—	—	music therapy	—	—	—	—	—	_____
—	—	—	—	—	mutual story telling	—	—	—	—	—	_____
—	—	—	—	—	perception checking	—	—	—	—	—	_____

Note. Adapted from "Techniques used in counseling and psychotherapy" by J. W. Hollis, 1980, in *Practicum Manual for Counseling and Psychotherapy* (pp. 80-83) by K. M. Dimick & F. H. Krause, 1980, Muncie, IN: Accelerated Development. Copyright 1980 by Accelerated Development. Adapted by permission.

COUNSELOR'S OUTLINE FOR
ASSESSMENT OF BEREAVED CHILD

The following outline has been useful in assessing the bereaved child's needs. The sequence and the inclusion or exclusion of data is easily adjusted to the individual situation.

Identifying Information: Name, age, sex, address, school, grade.

Referral Source/Information: A brief statement giving reason for referral and referral source (i.e., parent, teacher, physician).

Factors Related to the Death Itself: A brief statement of nature of the death, child's relationship to the dead person, the "meaning" of the death to the child.

Parent and Family Information: Structure; origins; interrelations of family members; and social, economic, and cultural status of family.

School History: Progress and achievement in, and adjustment to, school and its programs.

Medical History: Serious illnesses, injuries, operations, physical disabilities, and general medical condition.

Psychometric Evaluation: Cognitive and projective assessment.

Interests and Special Abilities: List of interests and special abilities that may be helpful in involving the child in meaningful activities.

Interpersonal Relations: Attitudes toward self and others both past and present. Note any significant changes since the experience of death.

Synthesis and Recommendations: Summarize available information and perceptions of child and family; impressions of grief response; recommendations and counseling plan.

Prognosis: A predication of probable outcome.

SUMMARY GUIDELINES AND
GENERAL SUGGESTIONS
CONCERNING CHILDREN AND GRIEF

1. *Be a good observer.* Receptively attend to a child's behavior by maintaining eye contact and a responsive posture. Usually more growth occurs in exploring questions than attempting to provide quick answers.

2. *Respond in an empathetic manner.* Make your baseline helping response the reciprocal empathetic understanding, acknowledging the explicitly expressed feelings of the child and reasons or experience behind them.

3. *Allow the child to express feelings and thoughts.* Do not attempt to "over understand" the child, particularly in fields related to psychological data. It is better to allow the child to communicate depth of understanding to you, rather than attempting to "diagnose" what the child is thinking and feeling.

4. *Respond to the child in language that he/she can understand.* Be simple and direct. Begin at the child's level and remember that attitude is more important than words. What is said is not as important as the emotional meaning communicated to the child.

5. *Respond to the impact of events on the child (internal frame of reference) rather than to external facts only.* Remember—reality is for the child the world as he/she perceives it.

6. *Respond in a voice, tone, and intensity that reflect the affect expressed by the child.*

7. *Develop your skill in recognizing and responding to minimal cues of the child.* Check out the accuracy of your understanding with the child, but in such a way that the child can modify or change your perceptions in the reaction. If you are aware that the child is experiencing feelings, even though your awareness is from the child's nonverbal behavior, feed this back to the child in a supportive, nonthreatening permissive manner.

Caregiving Aspects of Helping the Grieving Child   89

8. *Express your own feelings that are natural to the situation.* This will provide the child with a basis for expressing feelings.

9. *Accept the child's questions.* Do not try to attach adult meanings to the child's questions. Usually the child's questions are quite simple and factual.

10. *Be patient and available.* Do not expect a child's reaction to the experiences of death to be obvious and immediate.

11. *Provide reassurance through action as well as words.* Remember—the child is part of the family. Reassurance comes from the presence of loving people. Children feel secure in the care of gentle arms and loving tenderness.

12. *Learn to tolerate and feel at ease during reasonable periods of productive silence.* Generally speaking, acceptance, reflection, and silence often result in increased understanding. Oftentimes the child needs permission to talk at his/her own pace, not to be talked to.

13. *Maintain a continuing dialogue with children about death as the opportunity arises* (i.e., death of a pet, news events). Do not wait or plan for "one big tell-all."

14. *Create a healthy relationship between you and the child.* Recognize your helping-healing ambition and attempt to create a relationship with the child which is basically a healthy one.

15. *Select and adjust your procedures according to the child.* Remember—no one procedure or formula will fit all children, either at the time of a death experience or during the period that follows.

REFERENCES

Bebensee, B. A., & Pequette, J. R. (1982). *Perspectives on loss: A manual for educators.* Evergreen, CO: Author.

Combs, A. (1967). *Florida studies in the helping professions.* Gainesville: University Press of Florida.

Hollis, J. W. (1980). Techniques used in counseling and psychotherapy. In K. M. Dimick & F. H. Krause, (Eds.), *Practicum manual for counseling and psychotherapy,* (4th ed.) (pp. 80-83). Muncie, IN: Accelerated Development.

Reik, T. (1948). *Listening with the third ear.* New York: Grove Press.

Walters, R. P. (1975). *The amity book: Exercises in friendship and helping skills.*

SUGGESTIONS FOR FURTHER STUDY

Brammer, L. (1973). *The helping relationship.* Englewood Cliffs, NJ: Prentice-Hall.

Brammer, L. & Shostrum, E. (1977). *Therapeutic psychology: Fundamentals of counseling and psychotherapy* (3rd ed.). Englewood Cliffs, NJ: Prentice-Hall.

Carkhuff, R. (1972). *The art of helping.* Amherst, MA: Human Resource Development.

Gazda, G. M. (1973). *Human relations development: A manual for educators.* Boston: Allyn and Bacon.

Gordon, T. (1970). *Parent effectiveness training.* New York: Peter H. Wyden.

Gray, H. D., & Tindall, J. (1978). *Peer counseling: An in-depth look at training peer helpers.* Muncie, IN: Accelerated Development.

Ligon, M., & McDaniel, S. (1970). *The teacher's role in counseling.* Englewood Cliffs, NJ: Prentice-Hall.

Rogers, C. (1951). *Client-centered therapy.* Boston: Houghton Mifflin.

Chapter **5**

PREPARING TO HELP OTHERS HELP CHILDREN

Some of you may choose to develop programs aimed at educating your community regarding the topic of "Helping Children Cope With Grief." If so, you will find that your efforts to develop effective coping resources within your community, to better help meet the social and psychological needs of children during this vulnerable period, will depend largely on your own efforts.

In your efforts to build a cooperative relationship among community service agencies, you will find a large amount of time will need to be spent visiting various professional and lay people in your community. The time has come for the concerned people in the community to make it happen; to move in positive directions. Action must replace talk, and most importantly, learning and growing must occur in areas where, to date, little if any progress has been made.

The content of this chapter is designed to assist you as you begin your efforts to develop a program focusing on community education related to *Helping Children Cope With Grief.*

PREPARING YOURSELF
TO BE A DISCUSSION LEADER

You have just received a phone call from the principal of a local grade school. He would like you to come to their next Parent Teachers Association meeting to talk about children and grief and to follow your presentation with a discussion among those present. This meeting is your opportunity to become a community educator who can assist others to help children cope with separation and loss. You agree to present the program and lead a discussion, but, to be honest, you are a little scared. You ask yourself, "Where do I go and what do I do now?"

When someone calls on you to speak to their group, a number of important questions to ask include the following:

     1. What is the nature of the group making the request? (Who are they?)

     2. Why do they want me to talk about children and grief? (Why are they interested?)

     3. What sources of information are available to me for presentation? (What tools are available to assist me?)

     4. What material or literature can I leave with them or show them? (What can they take home with them?)

     5. What shall I say? (Prepare and develop a plan.)

You might choose to use the Community Education Worksheet format to gather information from the person or agency requesting you to present a program. A copy is presented in Figure 5.1.

PREPARING FOR DISCUSSION

Much of everyday living consists of communication with other people, either singly or in small or large groups. Communicating with others is not simply a question of talking to them; it also involves an understanding of how they will receive your message.

COMMUNITY EDUCATION WORKSHEET

TYPE OF ACTIVITY: _____

FOR WHOM: _____

NUMBER IN GROUP: _____ AGE RANGE: _____

DATE: _____ TIME: _____ to _____

LOCATION: _____

TOPIC: _____

_____

WHO'S CALLING _____

PHONE: _____

ADDITIONAL INFORMATION: _____

_____

CALL REFERRED BY: _____

DATE: _____ TIME: _____

PERSON(S) WHO WILL PRESENT PROGRAM: _____

Figure 5.1. Community Education Worksheet for use in gathering information prior to making a presentation.

To begin to know others, you need to know yourself:

•How do you respond and react to communication of others?

•Have you taken the opportunity to reflect on your own experiences with death that occurred during both your childhood and adult years?

•How do you feel about asking others to contemplate issues related to death?

•Are you tense or at ease?

•How do you feel when you are a member of a group discussion?

Only you know how you will answer these questions. You can, with some certainty, gain from your answers the feelings people have about your communications with them. Ask other educators interested in children and grief how they might respond to these questions. This is not to say that others will feel exactly as you do; but instead, they may share a range of possible feelings, thoughts, and reactions, some of which will be similar to your own.

An essential step in developing your role as a community educator and group discussion leader is to develop a plan. Think of it like this: The quarterback of a football team does not just walk on the field during a game and wonder what to do. The quarterback has a plan. If the defense is set up in a certain way, any one of a set of certain offensive plays can be used. The quarterback's plan has a certain amount of flexibility determining play.

And so it can be with you. You have the ball and the opportunity to provide a meaningful learning experience to members of your community. The decision is up to you what you do with it. You are the quarterback of the group discussion. You should determine in your own mind what thoughts and feelings you think are important to share with the group:

•How might the group respond?
•What problems might arise?
•How is the group brought back to the subject if members detour? And
•What pertinent questions might be used to keep the discussion moving?

Anticipating problems and difficulties and having a "game plan" is better than to suddenly encounter a situation in the middle of speaking and begin wondering what you should do. Much of your leadership will consist of brief comments in response to questions or concerns. The more thought you give to the discussion before the meeting, the more informative and helpful you will be. In practical terms, results of a long period of preparation may be only a single sheet listing the main aspects you would like to cover during the discussion period, possible alternative viewpoints or questions, and possible illustrations. While this will take some time and effort on your part, you will most likely find that the benefit for the group and yourself will be well worth it.

IMPORTANCE OF PHYSICAL ARRANGEMENTS

Physical arrangements are often more important than we are aware. Part of your task as leader is to find a setting which helps the group feel at ease. Oftentimes you have no choice as to the type of accommodations, yet you can modify what you have so that it is as helpful as possible. Try to arrange chairs in a manner that will facilitate the flow of discussion—ideally with no one's back to anyone else. People both talk and listen more easily if they can see each other's faces, and a circle is by far the best formation. Room temperature should be comfortable. If it is too warm, many people will become sleepy. If too cool, people may be more concerned with their physical comfort than with the discussion. Keep in mind that the physical, as well as the emotional climate, will "set the mood" for your presentation and discussion.

A PRACTICAL NOTE

A practical measure for you to consider when the group is small enough or time allows is to provide an opportunity for introductions and contact between group members. Of course, this would be done only when the people within the group have not already had an opportunity to get to know each other. People tend to guard their conversation if they feel they are among strangers. In your role as discussion leader, you can allow them to get to know each other with just a little planning and forethought using information gathered in Activity 5.1.

SUGGESTED USE OF
THE FILMSTRIP

The filmstrip and accompanying audio tape entitled *Helping Children Cope With Grief* will be most useful for educating parent groups; human development classes at the high school level; groups involved in colleges, universities, and churches. It can be used by any individuals or groups interested in learning more about children and grief.

Helping Children Cope With Grief is a stimulus for thinking and more importantly for feeling. Therefore, follow-up activities are of great importance as they relate to the objectives of each group. Small group discussions and activities focusing on one or two points have proven to be exciting avenues for sharing reactions, ideas, and feelings, as well as for developing an increased awareness of needs of children at a time of a death. Specific activities are provided later in this chapter under the heading "Activities for Use in Discussion Groups."

GUIDELINES PRIOR TO
PRESENTING THE FILMSTRIP

Much of what is learned from the film and audio tape is not solely the content of what is presented, but rather are the emotional, intuitive, and humanistic aspects of the learning process. As a result, you will want to do everything possible to let those viewing the filmstrip do so in the best possible way. The tone you set from the onset and the specific viewing situation will have a tremendous effect on the audience response. Keeping this in mind, you may want to review, from time to time, the following guidelines prior to presenting this filmstrip to groups in your community.

1. Be sure that you have personally viewed the filmstrip and heard the tape prior to using them with a group. By previously viewing the filmstrip you will be better able to anticipate questions and concerns your audience may have.

2. Make sure that both the filmstrip and audio tape are in good condition. Preview them for this purpose even though you

have seen the filmstrip. Make an extra effort to take good care of the filmstrip. Minimize your handling of the film; fingerprints show through.

3. If you have not done so, become familiar with the operation of the filmstrip projector. Operation of this equipment is not difficult, but time is required to read directions and to practice the operating steps until the basics are mastered.

4. Before you start the filmstrip, be sure that the projector and audio equipment are working properly. If someone else is operating the equipment, check that they are thoroughly familiar with both the projector and the process of projection. Have an extra lamp ready and become aware of the projectors normal running sound so you will know if a problem arises.

5. Have the projector and screen all set up before time to use it. This includes the focusing of the filmstrip and having the audio tape set at the start of the audio sound. The most effective presentation is made by "just flicking a switch" and getting going.

6. Have the room as dark as possible to allow for the most effective projection of the filmstrip. However, good ventilation is more important than total darkness. A little light with circulating fresh air in the room is better than to have the audience uncomfortable.

7. Attempt to present this filmstrip to groups in an environment void of distracting noises. It can be distressing to be interrupted by outside noises.

8. If at all possible, arrange for the people viewing the filmstrip to do so from the best possible position as directly in front of the screen as possible. Remember, too, the greater distance between the projector and the screen, the larger the picture.

9. Stay in the room with the audience when you show the filmstrip and play the audio visual. Your visible presence communicates your concern and thoughtfulness.

10. Set an appropriate mood prior to showing the filmstrip. Tell the audience what it is about and attempt to personalize

your introductory comments to the individual group you are addressing. Your introductory remarks might include the purpose of the filmstrip; what to look for; why it is presented at this time; what they will learn from viewing it; and how they can apply the information gained.

The following is only a suggested list of audiences to whom you may wish to present the filmstrip and audio visual tape, *Helping Children Cope With Grief*. You may well discover other organizations and groups in your community who will have a desire to see this filmstrip, hear the audio tape, and have you speak to them.

> Teacher/Educator
> Parent Teacher Association
> Medical Caregivers
> Mental Health Workers
> Ministerial Associations
> Funeral Directors
> Church Related Organizations
> Service Clubs such as Jaycees or the Lion's Club and other service groups
> Community Organizations such as YMCA, YWCA, and others
> Interested Individuals and Families

In the space provided you may want to list specific groups in your community whom you might want to contact:

THE DISCUSSION SESSION

Obviously a long list of guidelines could be constructed for you to follow when serving as a discussion leader. However, attempts to follow a rigid set of instructions will not really help and may actually produce unnecessary tension for both you and the group with which you are involved. In your role as discussion leader, you should keep in mind some characteristics of effective discussion. You should examine suggested techniques in a common sense manner, asking if they will, in fact, help the specific group with which you are involved. With this in mind it may be useful to look at three main aspects of effective discussion behavior. These can be listed as follows:

1. getting the discussion started,

2. keeping it fruitful (i.e., helpful to learning) when it has started, and

3. providing a satisfactory ending.

Getting Started

Because what you will be discussing with group participants will most likely be new to them, it is important to provide some basic background information and to focus individuals' minds on the subject. An introduction also is appropriate from the standpoint that it allows people an opportunity to settle down and relax somewhat. It is vitally important to keep in mind that the longer the introduction, the more difficult it will be for conversation to begin; when people sit back to listen it requires more effort for them to change into active participants. Realizing this, you may want to pose a question or two to the group prior to showing the filmstrip. All in all, it is best to keep your introduction brief however make sure it achieves three objectives:

1. shows the purpose of your being there
2. focuses attention of the topic, and,
3. gives time for the group to settle down.

Keep Information Fruitful

After you have shown the filmstrip and the discussion has begun, part of your task as leader will be to make the session as helpful and informative as possible to those present. People need time to put their thoughts into words. If you encounter silence, you should not rush in too quickly, as you might interrupt the thought process and tempt some people to leave all of the talking to you. Attempt to sense whether the silence is caused by people having nothing to say or whether it is just a pause while they put their thoughts together. It is a fact that the more control you as leader and resource person exert, the less communication flow between those present. People learn best and are most receptive to new information when they are actively involved. Your awareness of this will help you to create a situation where everyone feels free to participate. In your role as discussion leader you will at times find yourself in a position where it will be helpful to clarify what people have said. Clarifying is bringing vague material into sharper focus. Examples of the use of clarifying follow: "I lost you; could you go over that again?" "You seem to be saying..." or "Do you mean...?" This will allow everyone to have an increased understanding of what is being said. It also communicates to people that you are trying to understand their basic message. You are *listening* to them, which makes them aware of your concern. State your clarifying remarks in terms of your own feelings of confusion, thereby avoiding implications of criticism.

Providing A Satisfactory Ending

Bringing your presentation and discussion to a satisfactory ending is a matter of personal judgement, depending upon the particular situation. In many situations, you will have a certain amount of time to present your total program. In general, it is better to close when people are still interested in learning more than to allow the session to grind slowly to silence. In concluding, you may find it appropriate to review briefly what has been discussed. Usually this means a restatement of the main points which have been made. When appropriate, you can stress the importance of the way in which participants have helped each other by testing out ideas, information, and experiences as well as hopes and fears.

This filmstrip contains much information to absorb in a short period of time. As a result, it is vitally important that you allow your audience to process that information immediately after showing it. The advantages of a follow-up discussion period involving questions and answers and sharing of thoughts and feelings cannot be overemphasized.

Perhaps the most important part of any follow-up discussion is to allow for individual exploration of thoughts and fears related to death. In providing an atmosphere for increased self-understanding, discussions frequently include talk of how one's own attitude toward birth, life, and death affects one's explanation of death to children. As was previously stated, adults can do much to help children at a time of a death experience, but not until they have examined their own thoughts and feelings. There is a real need for people who want to be of help to children to explore the acceptance of their own emotionality. Adults need to have a real awareness of their individual fears and limitations in helping children during this experience.

ACTIVITIES FOR USE IN DISCUSSION GROUP

The following structured activities are intended to enhance group participants' self-awareness and emotional freedom related to the topic of children and grief. The adult who attempts to be of help to children experiencing grief faces the implication of his/her own death and deaths of significant persons in life. Without awareness and active acceptance of one's own fears, the adult is likely to become anxiously over involved or maintain an emotional distance that precludes an effective helping relationship. Honesty and respect for our own personal feelings will make us more effective helpers to children at a time of loss.

A concern I have regarding the use of these structural activities is the need for adequate processing of experiences so that participants are able to integrate learning about self and others without stress that evolves from unresolved feelings and understanding about the activity. Related to this activity is the experience of the discussion leader, if the exercise is to be responsive to the learning and emotional needs of the participants. The discussion leader must decide his/her capability in appropriately processing the information that will grow out of experiences. Any discussion leader, with proper forethought, who is committed to the task of helping adults become better prepared to help children who experience loss can usefully apply these structured activities. The choice of particular activities should be based on two important criteria—the discussion leader's competence and the participant's needs.

In considering specific activities to include in this book, I have attempted to examine the specific needs of adult-helpers who will be helping children cope with grief and then to develop learning situations which will meet these needs. This concern for learning needs should be a minimum expectation of any person serving as a discussion leader. Therefore, objectives of each activity and the general procedures to be employed by the discussion leader are outlined. Following each activity is space to record your own notes about your reactions to the activity, or to write ideas about its usefulness to you as an adult learner. Of course, you can add activities that work for you, and omit some of the activities suggested.

ACTIVITIES: INTRODUCTORY NOTE

Prior to beginning these activities, state that at any time if a person does not want to participate in any of the activities, passing is certainly acceptable. The majority of people will usually take part in the activities; however, there are many reasons why persons may prefer not participating in an activity at any particular moment. For example, they might at that time be in touch with some deeply personal thoughts and feelings; they might believe that their comments would be irrelevant to the degree that they do not wish to share them with the group; they may have been thinking about other things and simply not know what is going on at that moment; or they might feel that anything they might add would only repeat what someone else has already said. While participation in the activity is very important, many people learn a great deal about themselves and others by observing and, for effectiveness, the participation must come when the person is ready.

In summary, before initiating activities you will want to reassure participants that you will not push or prod them into anything they do not wish to do and that they are free to decline involvement at any point. In doing this you model respect and acceptance of the participants.

Activity 5.1
GETTING ACQUAINTED: "WHO AM I"

Time Required

30 minutes

Goals

•To enable participants to become acquainted quickly or to become better acquainted if they already know each other.

104   *Helping Children Cope With Grief*

Group Size

Dependent on size of group, the entire group can participate or may need to divide into groups of five or six persons in each group. Any reasonable number of small groups may be accommodated.

Materials Utilized

Blank 4x6 cards, pencils, and straight pins for each participant

Procedure

1. Participants receive materials and are given 10 minutes to write the following on the card:

    a. Please call me:
    b. The age at which I first experienced a death was:
    c. One feeling I realize I had at that time was:
    d. If I were an animal I would like to be a:

2. Each participant pins the card on his/her clothing so that it may be read easily by another person standing face-to-face.

3. Participants begin to circulate around the room, reading each other's cards. This entire part of the activity is done without talking (about 10 minutes).

4. After this nonverbal experience, the leader directs participants to return to several different persons they think they would like to know better, based on what they have read in the nonverbal encounters. Participants may now speak with each other and are encouraged to ask questions related to the information on the cards. This part of the activity will take another 10 minutes.

Notes:

Activity 5.2
DRAWING A PICTURE OF DEATH

Time Required

30 minutes

Goals

•To stimulate thoughts and feelings related to death.

•To enable participants to get acquainted while focusing on the topic of death.

Group Size

Dependent on size of group entire group can participate or may need to divide into groups of five or six. Any reasonable number of small groups may be accommodated.

Materials Utilized

Paper and crayons

Procedure

1. Participants receive materials and are instructed to draw a picture of death. They have five to ten minutes to work privately in this phase.

2. After most participants finish, they hold their drawings in front of them and circulate around the room without speaking. (Ten minutes).

3. After this nonverbal experience, participants are asked to return to two or three people to talk about their drawings. Upon conclusion of the subgroup discussion someone representing each group tells the larger group about the various drawings depicting death.

Notes:

Activity 5.3
REFLECTION OF DEATH EXPERIENCES

Time Required

Approximately one hour

Goals

•To encourage recollection of early experiences with death.

•To determine rules that existed about death within one's family of origin.

•To recognize that anxiety in significant loss situations for others is frequently a reflection of our own fears related to these losses.

Group Size

Entire group or 5 or 6 in group

Dependent on size of the group an entire group can participate or may need to separate into groups of five or six. Any reasonable number of small groups may be accommodated.

Materials Utilized

Sentence Completion Inventory and pencil

Procedure

1. Each participant receives a copy of the Sentence Completion Inventory and instructions to complete it. Allow fifteen to twenty minutes to work privately at this point.

2. Upon completion of the inventory participants are seated in one large circle and the discussion leader selects various sentences and asks people if they will share their responses.

3. These sentences serve as stimulus material for thoughtful discussion. The discussion leader simply uses personal judgement before asking the next question.

Preparing to Help Others Help Children   107

SENTENCE COMPLETION INVENTORY REGARDING CHILDREN AND DEATH

Time Required

20 to 30 minutes

Please complete each of the following incomplete sentences. There are no good or bad, right or wrong answers.

1. My first experience with death was

2. Right after this first experience I felt

3. My primary source of emotional support during childhood was

4. When death occurred in my family, my parents

5. The biggest rule my family had about death was

6. When I was a child, the worst thing about death was

7. When I think about my experiences with death as a child, I realize

8. The needs I had as a child when a death occurred, were as follows

9. Talking to children about death is

10. When I think about children and funerals, I

11. When people talk about children and death fifty years from now

12. We teach children that death is

Notes:

Activity 5.4
EXPRESSION OF FEAR RELATED TO
TALKING TO CHILDREN ABAOUT DEATH

Time Required

20 to 30 minutes

Goals

•To recognize that our anxiety in significant loss situations for others is often a reflection of our own fears related to these losses.

•To recognize that our anxiety in significant loss situations for others is often a reflection of our own fears related to these losses.

Group Size

Entire group or small groups of 5 or 6 in each group

Dependent on size of group, an entire group can participate or may need to separate into groups of five or six. Any reasonable number of small groups can be accommodated.

Materials Needed

Pencil and list of incomplete sentences

Procedure

1. Each participant receives a copy of the following incomplete sentences:

I am comfortable in talking to children about death because

I am uncomfortable in talking to children about death because

I would rate my fear of talking to children about death as follows:

1   2   3   4

No Fear   Low Fear   Moderate Fear   High Fear

2. After each participant has completed the information requested in 1., they are asked to discuss their fear or lack of fear of talking to children about death. The discussion leader should encourage people to talk about "whys" connected to their fears. Likewise, those people who believe they have no fear of talking to children about death also should be asked to talk about the "whys."

Notes:

Activity 5.5
A REMEMBRANCE OF CHILDHOOD LOSSES

Time Required

Approximately 30 minutes

Goals

•To enable participants to review a variety of loss experiences from childhood.

•To create an opportunity to recognize naturally occurring developmental losses.

Group Size

Small groups of five or six

Materials Utilized

Writing paper and pencil

Procedure

1. Participants are invited to "brainstorm" a list of possible losses experienced as a child growing into adulthood. Participants are encouraged to think of personal experiences as well as observation of others.

2. Upon completion of the list, participants are asked to discuss those losses they found most difficult with which to cope and why they were so difficult. The discussion leader simply uses personal judgment as to when to conclude discussion.

Notes:

Activity 5.6
LOOKING INTO THE PAST

Time Required

Approximately one hour

Goals

•To enable participants to recognize thoughts and feelings related to loss experienced during their childhood.

•To create an opportunity to empathize with a child's phenomonenological experience of coping with the emotions of grief.

Group Size

Dependent on size of group entire group can participate or may need to divide into groups of five or six. Any reasonable number of small groups may be accommodated.

Materials Utilized

Writing paper and pen

Procedure

1. Participants are invited to write a letter to a significant person from their past who died during the participants' childhood. Participants are instructed to write to these persons focusing on the following questions:

> a. What special memories do you have, both good and bad of the relationship?

> b. What special memories do you think this person, if alive, might have of you?

c. Write about the different emotions you had when this person died.

d. What memories do you have of this person's funeral?

e. Describe briefly to the person who has died what you have done with your life since their death.

f. If the person could answer back, what are some of the questions you might ask of them?

Allow participants thirty minutes to write this letter.

2. In groups of five or six participants discuss what they have included in their letter and what this activity was like for them. Special attention should be given to the emotions experienced at the time of the person's death; the significance of memories of their relationship with the person; and memories of the person's funeral. The discussion leader simply uses judgment as to when to conclude the follow-up discussion.

Notes:

Activity 5.7
PROJECTING A LIFE-LINE

Time Required

30 minutes

Goals

•To create an opportunity to think about one's life and the direction it has taken in the past and is taking, present, and in the future.

•To encourage personal death awareness.

Group Size

Dependent upon size of group entire group can participate or may need to divide into groups of five or six. Any reasonable number of small groups may be accommodated.

Materials Utilized

Large sheets of newsprint and pen

Procedure

1. Participants are invited to draw their own personal life-line illustrating significant events. They are told that they can do what they wish in symbolizing their life-line. In addition, they are instructed to place a mark at the point on their life-line where they see themselves today. Allow participants 5 to 10 minutes to complete this task.

2. In groups of five or six have participants discuss their life-lines. Suggest that they might want to consider the following questions:

   a. What is it that you have drawn?

b. What does your life look like at this point in time?

c. Where have you been?

d. Where are you going?

e. When will your life end?

The discussion leader simply uses judgment as to when to conclude the follow-up discussion.

Notes:

Activity 5.8
CREATING AN EPITAPH AND EULOGY

Time Required

Approximately one hour

Goals

•To allow for exploration of how one would like to be remembered.

•To provide an opportunity to explore one's life as well as one's death.

Group Size

Dependent on size of group entire group can participate or may need to divide into groups of five or six. Any reasonable number of small groups may be accommodated.

Materials Utilized

Writing paper and pen

Procedure

1. The participants are invited to write their personal epitaphs and eulogies. The discussion leader describes an epitaph as being a short statement or quote that the participant would want displayed on his/her tombstone. The eulogy is described as a written message that the participant hopes might be said upon his/her death. The date of death may be projected far into the future, so the person may want to include activities planned but not yet accomplished. The eulogy should include the following information woven into an interesting story form—a story of one's life, happenings, contributions, other details of interests to loved ones and friends.

    a. age at death

    b. cause of death

c. circumstances of death

d. what person is best remembered for

e. whom he/she is survived by

f. details of the funeral and burial

g. any additional information

Allow approximately 20 minutes to work privately at this point.

2. When all participants have completed their epitaphs and eulogies, the discussion leader encourages participants to discuss their epitaphs/eulogies, focusing on the thoughts and feelings they had as they wrote these. Each participant should be allowed an opportunity to add to the discussion. The discussion leader simply uses judgment as to when to conclude the activity.

Notes:

Activity 5.9
GROUP EXPLORATION:
EXPERIENCING LOSS AND CHANGE

(NOTE: The suggestion is that only experienced leaders attempt this activity.)

Time Required

Approximately 30 minutes

Goals

•To allow for an explanation of personal patterns of coping with loss and change.

•To sensitize oneself to how others cope with loss.

Group Size

Eight to twelve participants are ideal however larger groups can also be accommodated.

Materials Utilized

Group Exploration Script

Procedure

1. The discussion leader invites the group to participate in an exploratory trip. He/she asks them to make themselves as comfortable as possible and to close their eyes. NOTE: A carpeted room where participants can recline and stretch out comfortably without restricting the space of others is ideal.

2. The discussion leader explains that guidance will be given to them through this experience and that they will simply want to listen and attempt to fantasize their experiences. The guide or leader tells them that from time to time questions will be asked. They are to answer these in their own minds, and they will be given the opportunity to express them openly in the groups when the experience has been completed.

3. The script entitled Group Exploration Script following this Activity should be read slowly in a caring tone of voice.

4. Upon completion of this activity the discussion leader asks participants if they would like to explore their reaction to the experience. While participants should not be pushed, they can be reinforced for using the opportunity as a learning experience.

Notes:

GROUP EXPLORATION SCRIPT

"I would like for you to take a trip backward in time, to the time when you left your family to go out into the world on your own. Try to remember as much as you can about that experience. How old were you at that time? Had you just graduated from high school, or did you leave home before or after that time? Take your time, but try to get a picture of that day in your life when you left home (brief pause).

"You may not think you remember that particular time in your life but feel your body. Allow yourself to experience those feelings. What were you feeling? Were you scared? excited? angry? happy? sad? How did you feel? What did you experience?

"This was a major turning point in your life. It was a major phase of moving into the adult world. How did you handle it? Did you repress your feelings or did you express them? What did you feel and what did you do? (brief pause).

"As you realize, each individual copes with turning points in life very differently. Some are supported in times of loss and change, others are crushed by change, or not allowed to recognize that loss and change have occurred. What has been your experience?

"I'm going to be quiet for a few minutes and I want you to visualize how you end things in your own life. How do you end relationships? How do you wind up a phase in your life? I would like for you to be able to visualize and think about one important ending in your past. Perhaps the end of a relationship as a result of death or divorce. It may be the end of being single and the beginning of married life. How did you say good-bye to someone in your life? It might be a move or a change in job. Whatever it is, I want you to re-experience thoughts and feelings you had at that time (pause).

"Whatever the experience might be that you choose—did you express your feelings or did you deny them? Did you withdraw or share your feelings? Do you usually end things in pretty much the same way? (pause)

"Become aware of where you are—realize that there are many possible ways to experience a life transition. By thinking about and becoming more aware of your own pattern of endings, you probably will find that you become more sensitive to the pattern of those around you.

"In just a few moments you want to bring yourself back totally and completely to this room and to the present. As you experience this, just allow your eyes to come open."

Activity 5.10
DIMENSIONS OF OPENNESS AND HONESTY: PROVIDING FOR EXPRESSION

Time Required

30 to 45 minutes

Goals

•To explore the dimensions of openness and honesty as related to talking to children about death.

•To promote the expression of openness and honesty with children at a time of a death experience.

Group Size

Dependent on size of group entire group can participate or may need to divide into groups of five or six. Any reasonable number of small groups may be accommodated.

Materials Utilized

Writing paper

Procedure

1. The discussion leader expands on the concepts of openness and honesty as presented in the filmstrip *Helping Children Cope With Grief.* The focus is on the idea that although parents, teachers, and counselors often acknowledge the need for openness and honesty in helping children cope with grief, the difficulty occurs in relating terms to feelings involved in the expression of openness and honesty.

2. The discussion leader forms small groups of five or six participants each.

3. The facilitator then instructs the groups to concentrate on what elements, feelings, and behaviors are involved in communicating openness and honesty to children at a time of the death experience. Participants should then be encouraged to explore these ideas thoroughly with one another. The discussion leader asks participants to "brainstorm" a list of these specific ideas to present to the group as a whole.

4. When all groups have finished, the facilitator asks one member from each group to make a presentation of the list of ideas.

5. When the participants have finished their presentations, the discussion leader asks them to select those ideas that they feel best communicated the concepts of openness and honesty.

6. The discussion leader assists in processing this activity by asking group participants to explain why the ideas selected are appealing.

Notes:

Activity 5.11
GROUP QUESTIONNAIRE RELATED TO CHILDREN
AND DEATH EXPERIENCES

Time Required

20 minutes

Goals

•To allow participants to compare and contrast attitudes related to children and death experiences.

Group Size

Entire Group

Materials Utilized

"Questionnaire Related to Children and Death Experiences"

Procedure

1. Each participant receives a copy of the "Questionnaire Related to Children and Death Experiences" and is instructed to complete it. Allow approximately 10 minutes to work privately at this point.

2. When questionnaires have been completed, the discussion leader collects the questionnaires. If additional group meetings will be held, the leader will tabulate from the questionnaires the groups's attitudes prior to the next meeting and at that meeting present the findings to participants.

3. Each item can be discussed individually and attitudes explored with the entire group. The discussion leader simply uses judgment as to when to conclude the discussion.

Notes:

QUESTIONNAIRE RELATED TO CHILDREN AND DEATH EXPERIENCES

Directions: Read each statement carefully. Circle the response which most clearly describes your level of agreement.

Strongly Agree (SA)
Agree (A)
Disagree (D)
Strongly Disagree (SD)

A parent should:

1. Feel uninhibited in sharing personal beliefs about death with children.	SA	A	D	SD
2. Encourage and aid in the normal mourning process within children who have experienced a significant personal or family loss.	SA	A	D	SD
3. Leave death education to the school.	SA	A	D	SD
4. Tell children something you may not believe in an effort to protect them from the emotions of grief.	SA	A	D	SD
5. Set a specific timetable for the resolution of children's grief.	SA	A	D	SD
6. Recognize the function ritual contributes to the child's grief process.	SA	A	D	SD
7. Explain that a dead bird or fish is sleeping.	SA	A	D	SD
8. Set a specific age at which you begin to discuss death with children.	SA	A	D	SD
9. Help children recognize that both happy and sad feelings are a normal part of life.	SA	A	D	SD

10. Leave death education to the church and/or church-related programs for children.　　　　SA　A　D　SD

11. Develop an understanding of children's perceptions of death at each developmental level.　　　　SA　A　D　SD

12. Try to understand exactly what children are asking about death.　　　　SA　A　D　SD

Activity 5.12
CLOSURE EXPERIENCE

Time Required

15 minutes

Goals

•To allow for a sense of having gained new information as a result of participation in a discussion session.

•To provide a sense of closure to the activities.

Group Size

Dependent on size of group entire group can participate or may need to divide into groups of five or six. Any reasonable number of small groups may be accommodated.

Materials Utilized

Closure Experience Worksheet

Procedure

1. Each participant receives a copy of the Closure Experience Worksheet and is instructed to complete it. Allow approximately 5 minutes to work privately at this point.

2. The information gained serves as a stimulus for what people will take away from the experience and encourages continued thought related to the issues of children and grief. The discussion leader simply uses judgment about concluding this activity.

Notes:

CLOSURE EXPERIENCE WORKSHEET

The most helpful aspect of this discussion for me has been...

Something I have learned about myself has been...

Right now, I'm feeling...

Two people with whom I would choose to explore this topic more would be:

1.

2.

DISCUSSION QUESTIONS

The following questions are intended to serve as a stimulus for follow-up discussion after presenting the filmstrip *Helping Children Cope With Grief.*

1. How has the isolation and separation of our older adults from our young people affected the child's perception of death?

2. How do children become really aware of their parent's feelings at a time of a death experience? Should parents hide their feelings at this time?

3. Should parents discourage their children from expressing their feelings?

4. What are some of the different reactions a child might have when a death occurs?

5. Should children be included in making arrangements for the funeral? Should they be allowed to attend the funeral?

6. Explain and discuss the four factors outlined in the filmstrip that are said to be helpful to children in their journey through grief (Ritual, Feelings, Facts, and Time).

7. Explain the importance of facts with children concerning death experience.

8. How can parents and other significant adults assist the child in his/her attempts to express grief?

9. Explain why children may differ in their reactions at a time of death in a family.

10. How does the funeral assist in helping children move through the grief process?

11. Is it important that parents give the child an honest explanation of death? If so, how can this best be accomplished?

12. Do children sometimes have feelings of guilt and responsibility for the death of the one they love?

13. Why do parents sometimes find it difficult to talk with their children about death?

14. To what extent do adult's values affect our capacity to explain God and heaven at a time of death?

15. What are some of the pitfalls that parents and other adults should avoid in their attempts to explain death to children?

GUIDELINES FOR PROGRAM DEVELOPMENT

The following guidelines are designed to assist those persons who wish to develop a program focusing on community education related to "Children and Grief."

1. *Do not try to do too much too fast.* There is only so much any of us can do. We can be available and attempt to help people learn about children and grief, but we cannot force them. The first step in community education is bringing about a sense of responsibility and attempting to provide a healthy atmosphere in which learning may take place.

2. Focus your efforts in the areas of your community which are most vulnerable; at the same time, keep in mind the needs of the total community.

3. If plans include cooperative services, they should be understood well in advance by those people involved and communicated in the most effective way to other community residents.

4. Let community agencies, as well as the general public, know what you can provide and provide only those services that you are well-qualified to give. Group presentations and referrals are always appropriate; direct counsel should be done only with specialized training.

5. When working with groups, allow for individual exploration of thoughts, concerns, and fears related to death, in an effort to demonstrate the significance of how one's attitude toward both life and death affects one's explanations and interactions with children about the death experience.

6. Provide and solicit sharing of a variety of reading materials concerning children and death for parents, teachers, clergy, medical personnel, and anyone else interested in learning more about this topic and the role of caregivers.

7. Recognize that initiation and coordination of vital services to the community provide the kind of leadership that is so desperately needed.

The development of such a program in your community can be difficult, slow, and even discouraging at times. Also, it can be enriching and fulfilling. However, if the important challenge to educate is not met, we will find that our children, when they reach adulthood, can be the victims of the same errors and lack of concern for others that have been evidenced in our present society.

Chapter **6**

QUESTIONS
AND ANSWERS

Over the past several years I have collected questions that workshop participants have asked. The following questions are representative of those asked and for each a brief answer is given. A review of these questions may help you analyze areas of concern to others. Often comfort can be gained in recognizing that others have many questions too. If a question is similar to one you have, then read the answer provided to gain ideas. My hope is that you, the reader, will understand that I am making suggestions, not giving instructions. As a caregiver your primary tool is yourself and because we are all unique we are all using different tools.

Question: *Could you expand on the child's expression of grief through physical illness?*

When children feel shut off from avenues of emotional expression of their fears, questions, and concerns, the not infrequent consequence is that they become physically ill. The child who is sick as a result of unexpressed thoughts and feelings does not consciously want to be sick—and certainly does not feel in control of his/her illness. The aches and pains expressed frequently are very real and they do hurt. The child's mind and body are inner related and they influence each other in ways that both the child and adults have little understanding. This type of illness is most often referred to as "psychosomatic"—with psycho meaning mind and soma meaning body. While this type of illness often needs medical intervention, the unfortunate result is that this kind of care most often does not get to the cause of the child's fears and concerns. Nevertheless, a comprehensive medical examination should be done in an effort to rule out any physical problems that might have been overlooked.

When ten-year-old Sally Johnson came home from school with a stomachache three days in a row, her Mother sensed that besides the pain something else was bothering her. Fortunately, Mother called Sally's teacher and discovered that the children had been drawing pictures of their family during art class. Sally did not know if she should include her Father in the picture since he had died in an industrial accident six months ago. Mrs. Johnson and the teacher were able to discuss ways of helping Sally talk about and cope with this situation, and Sally decided that while her Daddy was no longer alive it was natural for her to want to include him in her family drawing so soon after his death. These drawings actually served as valuable methods for Sally to express her thoughts, feelings, and memories related to her Father. Gradually the pictures became easier for her to draw, and Sally's physical health improved. Eventually, she eliminated her Father from family drawings; however, she continued to include him in her memories. She no longer felt trapped and unaware of how to express her many thoughts and feelings.

Situations like Sally's are not always easily and quickly resolved. Anytime that physical symptoms continue over a period of time, both medical and psychological methods of help should be consulted in an effort to gain a comprehensive picture of the child's situation.

Question: *Shouldn't I try to provide an immediate solution to my children's questions when they experience a death in their lives?*

I find that those adults who believe it is their place to provide immediate solutions in responding to grieving children often tend to assume total responsibility for the child's thoughts and feelings, resulting in the reinforcement of the dependent role. Frequently, these role perceptions blind the child from seeing any strengths and prohibit development of new strengths. Reinforcing dependency often keeps the child from growing and at times actually encourages regression. If you do not know the answer to a specific question, or a question really cannot be answered, be honest with the child. Actually, a child's realization that adults don't know all the answers can be comforting and create an increased sense of bonding.

Question: *Ten months after the death of my wife, my nine-year-old son got the flu and became terribly afraid that he might die. I felt so helpless. How might I have dealt with this situation?*

What had your son been told about his Mother's death?

Well, she had a chronic illness (cancer) and I just told him she was sick and we couldn't prevent it, so she died.

Your question raises a number of important issues. Children's questions about their own death often reflect deeper fears, and it is difficult to know just how to respond. First of all, your son may at some level feel responsible for his Mother's death and feel that his illness and possible death are the means by which he is being punished. You will note that in your explanation to your son you stated "we couldn't prevent it, so she died." While you certainly did not intend it, the result may have been that your son felt that it was his job to have prevented the death. Guilt feelings like these present a difficult struggle when faced by the child alone. Children need reassurance to help them understand that they are not to blame in any way for the death, that they are safe, and that the remaining parent will continue to love and care for them. This example helps illustrate the kinds of worries that may lie beneath a child's questions. Oftentimes, parents unknowingly communicate to the child that they are in some way responsible for a parent's death. Reassurance that the child is not to blame may have to be repeated over and over again—in different ways and at different times, because young children find death difficult to comprehend all at once.

Bereaved children commonly express a fear of their own death, particularly during times of illness. The question, "Will I die, too?" may come as a shock to a parent who, even with the best of intentions, might respond by saying, "Don't be foolish," or "Don't even talk about things like that." An answer like this of course, is inappropriate, and does little to aid the child who is struggling with this overwhelming fear. The child may well remember that Mom was sick and she died. This illustrates the importance of being specific with children about the nature of the illness that caused the death of a parent or significant person in their life. Of course, the explanation would have to be given at the child's level of understanding.

Perhaps an example will be helpful in responding to your question. Nine-year-old Kim, restless and uncomfortable with the flu, asked her Mother anxiously if her flu was like Grandma's who had died three months ago. As her Mother provided her with a sense of physical comfort by holding her hand she said, "Grandma died from heart disease which is very different from the flu bug that you have. Grandma also was very much older than you and I are. Children who have your kind of illness can be helped by parents who love them very much and doctors who have medicines that help. Dr. Olson knows just how to help you get well and I am here to help too." Even if specific words don't always accomplish their purpose, the tone of a caring voice is likely to reassure the child. Fortunately, children also learn from experience that their illness does get better and they do get well again.

Frequently, children simply want to know you are there and can be counted on to help take care of them. Children also are likely to worry more if a sense of mystery surrounds their illness. Do not give your child the impression that you are trying to hide something but instead be open and honest about the medicines and treatment needed to enable him/her to get out and play as soon as possible. If a medical doctor is involved in the child's care, speak with the child in the presence of the doctor to prevent any suggestion of concealing information from the child.

Question: *After my husband died, my first urge was to move to another city, but my children really seemed to resist. What about a move after the death of a significant person in the child's life?*

My experience has been that it is best to maintain some consistency in the child's environment following a significant death. To make a move involves much more than just a loss of the home—but also the loss of friends, change of school, and change in a routine. To immediately add these burdens to the child's existing sense of loss only serves to complicate matters further. Both children and adults can be aided in the process of reconciliation by respecting the pace at which they make other changes in their lives. Of course, at times circumstances beyond control require that a move take place. When this lack of control is the case, let the child anticipate the move as opposed to thrusting this additional change all at once.

Question: *When our family dog died, my husband and I were amazed at the impact the death had on our children as well as ourselves. What thoughts do you have about the death of a pet?*

I find that the death of a pet is often the first opportunity that parents have to help their children cope with grief. By "opportunity" I mean it can be the event that initiates a healthy, open, and loving relationship of living and dying, or it can be the event that initiates an unhealthy, dishonest approach to living and dying.

Unfortunately, many parents attempt to replace the dead pet before the child has an opportunity to experience grief. While this is well-intentioned, it is actually more harmful than helpful. For the child the immediate thought is often that no other pet could ever replace the one that has died. The child is entitled to the opportunity to grieve the pet that was so much a part of life. After the passage of time, it can be appropriate to suggest finding another pet to share the same kind of love, but not to take the place of the previous pet.

Circumstances surrounding the death of a pet should be dealt with openly and honestly with the child at a level of understanding appropriate to age. The child can begin to learn of the finality of death by being helped to realize that the pet is dead and will not be back. Parents can model their own feelings of loss over the death of the pet and help the child realize that the child did not in any way cause the death.

Allowing and encouraging children to participate in funeral rituals for their dead pet is another way of allowing for the expression of grief. Children often conduct funerals for pets spontaneously, gaining comfort in the structure provided for their "grief work." Participation in the ceremony and burial often permits the child a sense of closure and provides a feeling of control during a difficult time. Parents can help by sharing in these moments and learning with the child rather than avoiding or denying what can be a very deep and rewarding experience.

Question: *Should we share our religious beliefs with our children?*

In sharing of religious beliefs with children, honesty is the most important consideration. Parents can only teach what they truly believe. Young children have a great difficulty dealing with philosophical abstractions. As a result, use simple words that the child can understand. The child need not and possibly cannot accept and understand the total religious philosophy of parents.

Many children naturally become frightened when they hear that after death people go to some poorly defined place. Upon the death of a child, I have known children who have heard from their parents or church pastor that God needed a little boy or girl in heaven, so the child was "taken." I have counseled with several children who were counting the days until they too would be "taken." Not too surprisingly, these children were having trouble sleeping and were experiencing generalized feelings of anxiety in their daily lives. This kind of misguided communication can have long-term damaging effects on the child's emotional well-being.

Even when you as a parent decide your child is capable of exploring religious concepts, do not feel guilty or ashamed if you cannot give exact definitions of God and heaven. Even the Bible only contains what God is *like*. Openness to mystery is valuable not only in answering children's questions about God, but also in approaching many occurrences in life with mystery and awe.

Question: *Should children be allowed to attend the funeral?*

For children, as well as adults, the ritual surrounding death is of great importance. The funeral is a significant occasion in the life of the entire family. The child should have the same opportunity and privilege as any other member of the family. Many authors attempt to set a specific age at which time a child should be allowed to attend the funeral. I find myself uncomfortable with this in that each child-family situation is different and calls for a different response to various needs. Ultimately, the child's attendance at the funeral should be dependent on whether or not the funeral will be helpful in coping with the experience of death. The behavior of adults, especially parents, during the period of the funeral is a tremendous influence on the child. If as a parent you are able to openly express thoughts and feelings and to help the child understand the naturalness of tears, you will do much to free the child to express a sense of loss at his/her own level. A barometer of your ability to make the funeral helpful to the child is often whether or not the child desires to attend. Children can often sense whether parents will be able to make the experience a meaningful and comforting experience and on that basis make a decision to attend or not attend.

Yes, the child should be allowed to attend the funeral, but never forced to go. By allowing the child to participate in the group sharing of a common loss, adults help in acceptance of reality and finality of death. A helpful approach is to explain in advance some of what the child will be seeing and where the family will be going. An area that parents often do not think of discussing with the child is the "why" of going to the funeral. We often talk about the fact that we are going, but fail to talk about why we are going. The funeral is a time to be together with family and friends, to gain support from each other. The funeral is a time to remember and affirm the life of the person who has died. The importance of sharing this with our children cannot be overemphasized.

The funeral is a significant occasion for the entire family. Ultimately, the child's attendance at the funeral is dependent on whether or not the funeral will be helpful in coping with the experience of death. Children can often sense whether parents will be able to make the experience meaningful and comfortable and on that basis will decide to attend or not attend.

The child's first visit to the funeral home can best be done with only a few people who are especially close. This will allow the child to react and show emotions more freely and to talk about feelings and concerns. The child should be encouraged to ask questions and provided opportunities to do so prior to, during, and after the funeral.

What about viewing the body? Keep in mind that children learn by watching adults' reactions. Adults should remember that children have no innate fears about the dead body. Viewing the body should not be forced on the child, but instead be a matter of choice. Some children want to see the dead person because what they imagine may be worse than what is real. Other children may not want to see the dead person at all.

The funeral can be a helpful tool in the child's adjustment to loss. To deprive one of involvement and belonging at this emotional time may well shake the sense of security and safety. Although children may not completely understand the ceremony surrounding death, they are likely to be effected by the sense of comfort, peace, order, and the feeling that life goes on.

Question: *How important are other family members regarding the child's ability to grieve?*

My experience has taught me that the significant adults in the child's life are *the most important factor* in allowing and encouraging the child to mourn. Several studies of children who have experienced the death of a parent have demonstrated that the remaining family members and the rest of the child's environment are critical determinants in the child's capacity to mourn (Furman, 1964). The child's ability to cope depends on the capacity of significant adults' expressing their own grief and conveying to the child that they can express a full spectrum of feelings. The sharing of grief between parent and child assists the family in recognizing both the uniqueness and commonality of their experience. This means that the child can learn that Mom or Dad is sad, but that this feeling is not a rejection of the child. When the child experiences that his/her parents are sad, but that this has nothing to do with the child, the result is that the child learns to freely express the full spectrum of feelings experienced.

Question: *Do I understand you to say that a parent's inability or lack of desire to talk about death can create problems for the child?*

Yes, most definitely. If we recognize that modeling is one of the primary ways in which a child learns, a parent teaches the child to repress feelings, not express feelings! The pain is healed through the expression of grief.

Question: *I recognized my daughter was having difficulty coping with the death of her Father, yet I hesitated to seek professional help. What do you make of this?*

Foremost is the importance of recognizing that seeking help for yourself or your child is not an admission of failure, but a testimony of love. Unfortunately, many parents view getting professional help for their child as an admission that they have failed in their parental responsibilities. This kind of thinking is also reinforced by a cultural environment that communicates that parents are to blame for any difficulties a child might have.

On occasions even the most sensitive and well-intentioned parent feels helpless in efforts to help the child cope with grief. Because of their own grief, parents may not have the emotional capacity to support the child working with grief. Recognizing this and seeking professional help is most often of tremendous benefit to both the child and the parent.

Question: *How can I as a parent explain to my child what going to a therapist or counselor means?*

I have found it helpful to explain the counselor or therapist's role as someone who works to help people feel better. The child's experience with an effective counselor usually helps support this explanation. The child can be helped to understand that in counseling the family can obtain help through playing and talking about their sad, angry, and hurt feelings.

Question: *Do you usually see a child in therapy alone or with the entire family?*

I find that frequently parents who identify a child as having difficulty are often having trouble with their own grief; as a result, I often ask to see the entire family in therapy. This serves several purposes. When a death occurs in the family, the entire family system is disrupted. While a specific child may demonstrate obvious symptoms, I find these symptoms are often a cry for help for the surviving parent or oftentimes for the entire family. While at times I do see children by themselves, I usually do so early in the therapeutic process and primarily for the purpose of psychometric assessment. My belief is that the therapist's role in family-oriented bereavement therapy is not to become a parent figure in the child's life, but to be a catalyst or facilitator and to help the parent incorporate the supportive role into the child's everyday experience. I find that the child then is able to transfer the positive feelings that develop for the therapist to the parent or other significant adult figure that has been involved in the therapy.

I also find the child being helped through experiencing parents desire to aid the child with many feelings. Often a child will perceive parents depression as a rejection of the child. With the aid of a counselor or therapist this perception can be corrected. When children are able to experience that the parent's sadness or anger is not because of them, the children realize they too can express a full range of feelings.

Question: *What kind of qualities should I look for in a therapist who could help my child with grief?*

In terms of training and experience, you should not hesitate to ask the therapist if previous work has been with children in the area of grief. Any qualified therapist will not be upset when questions are asked related to training. You as a parent are purchasing a service and as a result you should make every effort to obtain the best possible help available in your geographical area.

Beyond qualifications, you will want to feel as if the therapist is someone about whom you have positive feelings and whom you can trust. The therapist should be willing to discuss methods and goals of the process of therapy with you once a clear understanding is established of the nature of the difficulties. In that the outcome of therapy has a great deal to do with both the childs' and parents' willingness to participate actively in the process, I believe education is vital. Education in the sense that both parents and children know as much about the process and goals of treatment as the therapist does. After all, the child who understands what is being done and why in therapy develops a sense of participating in and working toward mutual goals.

Question: *I have heard you state that the "open-system family" is the family that is most capable of sharing grief with children. Could you explain this further?*

In referring to the "open-system family" I mean those families that permit and encourage the open and honest self-expression of its members. In such a family children are accepted as integral parts of the family and capable of understanding at their own level of development. Children are not seen as little, and as a result bad. In such a family, differences in terms of the meaning of the death are viewed as natural and are able to be discussed. In an "open-system family" children can participate in decision making; accept any and all feelings of grief; and say what they think and feel in that grief is viewed as an opportunity for growth.

Conversely in a "closed-system family" children are often encouraged to repress, deny, and hide their grief. The primary rule is that everyone in the family is supposed to think and feel the same way and as a result no need exists to talk about thoughts and feelings. In such a family, expression of grief is often impossible, and if it does occur, the expression is viewed as being abnormal or "sick." Children in this kind of family often carry their grief around with them for years and express it in various sorts of emotional and behavioral disturbances.

Question: *I am a school counselor and right now I am seeing an eight-year-old boy whose father died three months ago. During the last several weeks Gary has been afraid to go to school. I suspect he is afraid to leave his Mother fearful that something will happen to her, but I seem unable to get him to talk to me about this fear. Could you give me a specific suggestion on how to approach this topic with him?*

In similar situations I have had success in drawing the child out by using the Jimmy Green technique. This is when you as a counselor describe the child's fears as being similar to the fears of a hypothetical child, Jimmy Green. In doing this you indirectly give the child permission to feel feelings and to recognize the naturalness of these feelings. I find that children are much more receptive to this type of approach than being confronted directly about their fears. For example, I might say to the child: "You know, Gary, I knew a boy not very long ago that had a fear a lot like yours. His Dad had died too and he really got scared about going to school. Sometimes he would get a stomach ache or a headache and would tell his Mom he just didn't feel like going to school. This worried his Mom and she really didn't know what to do. Well, after this boy, Jimmy Green and I talked for awhile, we got an idea about what was bothering him. He was afraid that if he went to school and left his Mom alone that something might happen to her. He was so scared that he thought he better just stay at home with his Mom because he loved her very much and didn't want anything to happen to her. You know, Gary, it sounds like you might have some feelings like Jimmy Green did. Jimmy and I talked about his fears when we met together and after awhile it wasn't so scary for him to go to school. Do you think maybe you and I could talk like Jimmy and I did? I think we probably can."

In approaching the child in this way, you as a counselor can gain the child's attention and often encourage the child to share fears with you. This kind of technique can be used to test for a wide range of thoughts and feelings that you are aware the child is experiencing but having difficulty expressing.

Question: *Would it be misleading to use a child's name who doesn't really exist?*

Well, in reality there are many Jimmy Greens out there. The counselor who works with grieving children comes to know of children with similar fears. Using a specific name simply helps personalize your narrative to the child. Also, perhaps months later the child may ask the child's name that had a fear. When this question occurs the name Jimmy Green will come to mind. When working with girls, the name Joannie Green can be used.

Question: *How might you sum up the manner in which an adult evolves this "helping-healing-relationship" you talk about?*

To sum it up as briefly as I can, recognizing that at the same time this definition is not all-encompassing, would be to say that a "helping-healing-relationship" with a grieving child is when I comfort, I support, I empathize, I care, I understand—and once the child has resumed equilibrium I aid him/her to choose behavior that results in growth and future happiness.

Question: *As a school principal, I am interested in the kinds of qualities and knowledge that a teacher of death education should possess. Could you outline those qualities and knowledge?*

Dr. Daniel Leviton, the founding president of the Forum for Death Education and Counseling, responded well to your question when he outlined these following criteria for selecting the death educator

1. The teacher must have come to terms with his/her own death feelings and to have admitted not only to its existence but to its full status in the dynamics of his/her total personality functionings.

2. Teachers need to know the appropriate subject matter to be taught.

3. The teacher of death education needs to be able to use the language of death easily and naturally, especially in the presence of young. This is impossible for many people; however, most can probably learn to do it.

4. He/she needs to be familiar with the sequence of psychothanatological developmental events throughout life and to have a sympathetic understanding of common problems associated with them.

5. The teacher needs an acute awareness of enormous social changes that are in progress and of their implications for changes in our patterns of attitudes, practices, laws, and institutions concerning death. (Leviton, 1971, p.39).

Question: *Could you give an example children with whom you have worked and a method of gaining information related to their thoughts and feelings about a death that has occured?*

Yes, perhaps it would be helpful for me to share with you a specific child's experience and to demonstrate one of the ways I go about learning more about thoughts and feelings. Important to note is that I will be sharing only a very isolated portion of a more comprehensive evaluation. In addition, only a trained therapist should attempt to gather and interpret the following kind of information. The names, places, and dates included in this example have been changed to protect the identity of those persons involved. The one method of gaining information that will be demonstrated is the Tell-A-Story technique, in which the therapist is able to gain insights into the child's thoughts and feelings. Hopefully, the information gained provides a sense of direction in helping the child.

Identifying Information

Client's Name: Sara Smith
Address of Client: Indianapolis, Indiana
Name of Parent(s): Mr. and Mrs. John Smith
Chronological Age: 5 years and 11 months
Date of Birth: July 21, 1976
Sex: Female
Race: Caucasian
Educational Background: Finished kindergarten and two years nursery school
School: Central Elementary School
Date of Initial Interview: June 16, 1982
Examiner: Alan Wolfelt

Referral Source/Information: Sara Smith was referred for evaluation by her mother. Mrs. Smith reported Sara has appeared sad and withdrawn during the past three- to- four-week period. Mrs. Smith reports that Sara recently attempted to nurse off her, is asking to be carried frequently, and described numerous regressive behaviors. Mrs. Smith also described some recent difficulties with Sara's lack of feeling accepted and liked by peers.

Background Information: Sara Smith, an attractive five-year, eleven-month-old female, will be enrolled in the first grade in the fall of 1982. Sara lives with her mother, stepfather, and three-year-old brother, Steven. Sara's father, Larry, died June 6, 1981, as a result of suicide. The mother, Sally Smith, is 27 years of age, completed one and one-half years of college, and is employed as a factory laborer. She is currently pregnant, expecting a child in September. Sara's stepfather, John, age 30, is also employed as a factory laborer.

According to the mother, vision, audition, and speech are within the normal limits and developmental milestones were accomplished within the normal limits. The mother reports hand dominance is not definitely established, although she writes and eats with her left hand.

Although Mrs. Smith reported being ill twice during her pregnancy with Sara, the pregnancy and birth were unremarkable, with Sara weighing five pounds, eleven ounces at birth. Sara had eye surgery at nine months of age to open a tear duct. There is no history of serious illness, head injury, or convulsions. Mrs. Smith did remember one high fever when Sara was just an infant.

Mrs. Smith reported that Sara attended nursery school for two years prior to kindergarten. In January of this year, Mrs. Smith referred Sara for intelligence testing. She reported at that time that Sara was unhappy at school and preferred to play with her brother. The intellectual assessment indicated that Sara had an IQ of 120, which placed her in the superior range of general mental ability. She demonstrated strengths in the areas of general comprehension, vocabulary, verbal fluency, judgment, and reasoning.

TELL-A-STORY

(The following is a verbatim excerpt taken from a tape recording made during my interaction with Sara during one phase of my initial evaluation process.)

Alan Wolfelt: Once there was a girl who liked to...

    Sara: Play.

    A.W.: What did she like to play?

    Sara: -play with books -play with toys -sometimes her mother puts up her pony tails -she likes to put on her mother's shoes -she likes to turn on the lamp for her Mommy

    A.W.: Who did she like to play with?

    Sara: With a boy. They play hide-and-seek in the backyard.

    A.W.: And what is the boy's name?

    Sara: Tommy.

    A.W.: Who did she not like to play with?

    Sara: Her sister.

    A.W.: Why was that?

    Sara: Because she is big and she wants to be just like her sister.

    A.W.: One day this girl went out with her mother and father, and they got cross with her. What about?

    Sara: The mother got hit?

    A.W.: Why?

    Sara: Cause she didn't look both ways. She got hit and she got killed. She went in the graveyard.

    A.W.: Did anyone come to see her?

    Sara: Her daughter did.

    A.W.: What did her daughter say at the graveyard?

    Sara: (paused, got quiet) She said I love her and I don't want her to leave me.

    A.W.: What would the girl wish?

    Sara: I wish I had my Mommy back.

    A.W.: What happened then?

    Sara: Then she'd go away.

    A.W.: This girl had a friend she liked very much. One day she said, "You come with me and I'll show you something, but you can't tell anyone, because it's a secret." What did she show him?

    Sara: A cake.

    A.W.: What was the cake for?

    Sara: Her mother.

    A.W.: And why was that?

Sara: Because she loved her mother very much.
A.W.: When this girl went to bed, what did she think about?
Sara: Her mother and the cake.
A.W.: Why was that?
Sara: Because she loved her mother and didn't want her to leave her.
A.W.: One night she cried. What was the matter?
Sara: (long pause) Because her Daddy died.
A.W.: When she fell asleep, what did she dream about?
Sara: Outer space coming down.
A.W.: What did the outer space people say?
Sara: I want your lamp (looking at the lamp in the room).
A.W.: And what did the little girl say?
Sara: No, you can't have it.
A.W.: The girl woke up in the night. What made her wake up?
Sara: The outer space people, the lamp, and her Mommy and Daddy.
A.W.: One night she had a nice dream. A fairy came to her and said, "If you say what you really want, it will come true." What did she say she wanted?
Sara: A doll, a car, a pretty fluffy dress, a pretty fluffy apron.
A.W.: Did she want something from her Mommy and Daddy?
Sara: A baby doll. No, a real baby.
A.W.: What is going to happen after the baby comes?
Sara: Going to have to get rid of the boy baby.
A.W.: Anything else?
Sara: We'd have to get rid of the big girl.
A.W.: The fairy gave the girl a lot of money—$1,000. What did she do with it?
Sara: Bought a lot of stuff.
A.W.: What did she buy?
Sara: Some watermelon and a cherry tree.
A.W.: Before she went away, the fairy said, "You are growing up. Do you want to grow up?" What did she say?
Sara: No.
A.W.: Did she want things to stay just as they were or did she want anything different?
Sara: The house we used to live in.
A.W.: What did she want different?
Sara: Nothing.
A.W.: Did she want anything the same?
Sara: Everything the same as it was in the house we used to live in.

A.W.: What kind of end do we want to put on our story?
Sara: The girl's name is Cinderella and her last name is Snow White. I turn off the light and I go to bed. I go upstairs, and I go to sleep.
A.W.: What did you like about the girl in the story?
Sara: All of it.
A.W.: Is the girl like you in any way?
Sara: No.
A.W.: How are you different?
Sara: The little girl is a bat.
A.W.: And what are you?
Sara: I'm a person (smiles).

Tell-a-Story—Evaluation

Sara's story illustrates the strong identification with her Mother, as well as a fear of her Mother's dying and leaving her. There was a hint at the sadness connected to her Father's death; however, there also was a sense that this was something about which was not talked. There are some significant fears revolving around the birth of the expected child in September. Most notable is her fear that she will not be needed once the new baby is born. This in addition to her grief response (note that the evaluation was done shortly after the one-year anniversary of her Father's suicide) helps explain the regressive tendencies observed and reported by her Mother. This appears to be related to a fear of growing up and the desire for her life to return to the way it was prior to her Father's death. While she has not changed residences, she spoke of wanting to live in the house she used to live in. This, of course, was the home where her Father was present. She spoke very directly in terms of wanting everything the same as in the house they used to live in. Sara's generalized fears and anxieties are portrayed in her references to her dreams of outer space coming down. She also was able to communicate her sense of wanting everything to be all right, as indicated in her identification with Cinderella and Snow White.

These data were incorporated into the comprehensive evaluation that led to following recommendations:

1. Initiate play therapy, focusing on emotional expression, self-esteem, and dependency issues.

2. Initiate family therapy, focusing on the emotional needs of all family members, while at the same time aiding Sara in grieving the death of her father, to whom she had very close emotional ties.

3. Work with the Mother and Step-father to provide the means for Sara to get her affection and security needs met. Provide direct reassurance that Mother is in good health and both willing and able to care for Sara.

4. Encourage opportunities for Sara to become involved in enjoyable peer related activities, such as scouting, swimming, dancing, and so forth.

Hopefully, this helps illustrate one method of gaining additional insight into the phenomenological experience of the grieving child.

Postscript—I am pleased to report that Sara is living a very normal, healthy, loving life at this time.

Question: *I am aware that you have worked with the Compassionate Friends, an international organization of parents who have experienced the death of a child. Could you help me understand what it's like to be a member of that group?*

My hope is that the reprint of the following article will aid you in your understanding of the tremendous value of this self-help group for literally thousands of bereaved parents.

ON BEING A COMPASSIONATE FRIEND
Alan Wolfelt

In the midst of contemplating my thoughts, I was suddenly alerted to the man sitting next to me on the airplane asking, "Well, just what *is* The Compassionate Friends?" I paused, thinking of all the times I had been asked this question. "The Compassionate Friends is a self-help organization of bereaved parents," I answered.

And yet, in my relationship with this group over the past several years, I have come to realize what an inadequate response this is. To say anything more would require two things:

First, I would attempt to communicate more than the membership criteria. Secondly, I would try to put into words what The Compassionate Friends has given to me, both as a person and as a professional caregiver. (I am not a bereaved parent, and these observations are made from the outside looking in).

So, imagine that I have the ear of the man on the airplane and we start over again.

With a very interested look on his face the man asked, "Well, just what *is* The Compassionate Friends?"

I turned to my new friend. "Many people have discovered that our society puts a high value on being strong and repressing feelings—even when our lives have been intimately touched through the death of someone we love and who is a part of us. Friends and family may give the message that bereaved parents must hide their grief. How liberating it can be when people discover permission to express their innermost thoughts and feelings!

"Members of The Compassionate Friends *do* talk about the pain of their grief. Mutual expression of thoughts and feelings can bring about understanding and acceptance by others."

"You mean they actually talk about feelings that hurt?" he said, shifting uneasily in his seat. His question made me realize that in the context of receiving permission to be vulnerable and helpless, members are eventually able to provide support for others. Ironically, it is through the experience of helplessness that members can become helpful.

I replied, "No longer finding it necessary to 'be strong,' bereaved parents are able to share their mutual vulnerability without fear of being abandoned or rejected."

In the sharing of one's grief there is not only the discovery of the commonality of experience, but also the uniqueness of each parent's experience. The realization that one is not alone creates an aura of empathy and mutual caring for which there is no substitute. Upon recognizing part of one's experience in another person, thoughts and feelings become less strange. Mutual sharing provides an opportunity to explore with each other on deeper levels of understanding.

Moving to the edge of his seat, the man stated, "Yes, that sounds helpful, but it's awfully difficult for me to talk in front of others. Isn't it a struggle for them to say what they're feeling?"

"It does not take new members long to discover the healing nature of The Compassionate Friends. As more recently bereaved parents begin to experience the comforting pattern of open-ended group sharing, they are supported in moving *toward* their grief instead of away from it. A warmth and sense of hope evolves from the group interaction. Members are able to draw on each other's strengths. There is no message given that people must cover up their thoughts and feelings; on the contrary, they can express themselves openly in the presence of other bereaved parents. With this genuine caring, members experience a dimension of trust; they are able to share their pain with people they can 'count on.'"

"Parents are able to say to each other, 'Thank you for providing me a pathway by which I can rediscover myself.'"

I have witnessed that when small groups of members come together, the whole is greater than the sum of its parts. From the common bond that ties bereaved parents together evolves the highest kind of mutual support and understanding.

Being able to communicate one's feelings openly and honestly provides for a new way of communicating with oneself. Members are often able to respond more to the *depth of feeling* than to the words used. As bonds are established, specific words often become less important—parents come to know enough about each other to take shortcuts sometimes; they are able to sense each other's need for support. Emotional exchanges may be very concentrated; at other times, every-one needs a time-out.

The group learns that it can afford silences, and benefit from them, sitting quietly in the presence of others. From time to time, members are encouraged to silently contact the parts of their inner thoughts and feelings that may not otherwise be reached. And members learn that some of the deepest thoughts require time before they are ready and willing to surface—first into consciousness, then expression.

Of course, there may be people at a meeting who don't communicate one word verbally. Not speaking may simply be a way of saying that they are unsure of what they are feeling and do not wish to share it yet. Respecting the right to silence is another way of communicating support and understanding.

After a silence, the man turned to me. "It sounds like these people really get close to one another."

"Yes, many Compassionate Friends have discovered that through open communication there follows an enhanced self-understanding, and mutual growth that strengthens the bond between members. By realizing they are with others who understand, they are able to be more accepting of their own feelings, members arc able to become more familiar with the naturalness of those thoughts and feelings."

As the plane initiated its descent for landing I felt compelled to add: "I have gained much from The Compassionate Friends. Perhaps the most important thing I have experienced is the awareness that to receive total comfort I can't always wait for total acceptance before expressing my need for comfort. I guess The Compassionate Friends has helped me to keep in touch with and accept that vulnerable part of myself."

I have been helped to recognize that in my role as a "professional caregiver" I must work hard to maintain my humanness. Yes, my experience with The Compassionate Friends has helped me become more aware that when I share myself with others, I communicate my willingness to accept them as they are and my desire for them to accept me as I am.

As we touched down onto the runway, I added one thought. "Of course, not everyone's experience of what they gain as a Compassionate Friend is the same, nor should it be—and, most importantly, not until one has actually become a Compassionate Friend will he or she understand what the group provides."

"Well, just what *is* a Compassionate Friend?" As the years go by, I imagine the question will continue to be asked. My only hope is that I recognize the inadequacy of words when trying to convey what The Compassionate Friends is all about.

Reprinted with permission from *Thanatos, 7, 3.*

REFERENCES

Furman, R. A. (1964). Death and the young child: Some preliminary considerations. *Psychoanalytic Study of the Child, 19,* 321-333.

Leviton, D. (1971). The role of the schools in providing death education. In B. R. Green & D. P. Irish, *Death education: Preparation for living.* Cambridge, MA: Schenkman Publishing.

Wolfelt, A. (1982). On being a compassionate friend. *Thanatos, 7,* 3, 18.

Chapter **7**

CHILDREN AND GRIEF: CONTEMPORARY RESOURCES

In this chapter are provided additional resource materials to aid adults in efforts to help the grieving child. I have included the following:

1. A List of Selected Children's Literature Concerning Death;
2. Recommended Readings for Parents, Teachers and Counselors;
3. General Texts Focusing on Death and Dying;
4. General References: Journal Articles;
5. Selected Periodicals; and
6. Professional Organizations and Support Groups.

In recent years a number of death-related bibliographies have become available; the most comprehensive of these is entitled: *Death Education: An Annotated Resource Guide* (see general texts for reference). In this source are annotated more than 300 journal activities and books. The bibliography is subdivided into death education for children, for college students, for adults, and for health professionals and counselors. Detailed descriptions are provided for 28 selected textbooks and references. A list of 147 bibliographies and 67 references to measurement of death attitudes also is given. In addition, a list of audiovisual materials on death education (588 entries) and 99 organizations that are concerned with current issues in the death and dying field is included. This book is highly recommended as a general reference tool.

A LIST OF SELECTED CHILDREN'S LITERATURE CONCERNING DEATH

The following list is meant to give interested individuals a starting place in locating materials to help children learn in a meaningful way about loss, separation, and death. In addition to the appropriate age level, a short annotation of the material is provided.

A number of questions need to be asked when considering a particular book to be used with children. How does the book present the material—language, text, illustrations? What message would a child get from the book? How are feelings dealt with in the book? Are the content and language in the book appropriate for the developmental level of the child? How does the book define death? How could this book best be used with children? Does the book represent a general humanistic approach to death or a particular religious point of view? For specific guidelines in using books to aid children at a time of loss, see Joanee Bernstein's book, *Books to Help Children Cope With Separation and Loss* (see Recommended Reading for Parents, Teachers, and Counselors for reference).

Abbott, Sara. (1972). *The old dog.* Howard-McCann and Geoghegan. A boy's dog dies leaving him feeling empty. For ages 5 to 9.

Bartoli, Jennifer. (1975). *Nanna.* Harvey. Children take part in funerary rites and estate decisions after their grandmother's death. For ages 4 to 8.

Bernstein, Joanne. (1977). *Loss.* Seabury. A guide for young people who have lost someone close, touching upon practical and emotional aspects of death and its aftermath. For ages 10 and above.

Bernstein, Joanne, & Gullo, Stephen. (1976). *When people die.* Dutton. Life, death, and loss are investigated from the perspective of one woman's death. For ages 5 to 9.

Brooks, Jerome. (1973). *Uncle Mike's boy.* Harper and Row. A boy copes with the accidental death of his younger sister. For ages 8 to 11.

Brown, Margaret Wise. (1965). *The dead bird.* Young Scott. A funeral for a found bird. One of the classics in this field. For ages 4 to 8.

Buck, Pearl. (1958). *The beech tree.* John Day. The metaphor of a beech tree is used by an elderly man to explain his impending death. For ages Preschool to 7.

Cleaver, Vera, & Cleaver, Bill. (1970). *Grover.* Lippincott. The process of accepting a mother's suicide which she chose rather than a death from cancer. For ages 10 to 14.

Coburn, John. (1964). *Anne and the sand dobbies.* Seabury. A religious account of death as seen through the eyes of a young boy who loses his infant sister and dog. For ages 8 to 12.

Cohen, Barbara. (1974). *Thank you, Jackie Robinson.* Lathrop. The story of the relationship between a twelve year old boy and an elderly black cook who suffers a fatal heart attack. For ages 8 to 11.

Coutant, Helen. (1974). *First snow.* Knopf. Death as seen from the Buddhist point of view. For ages 5 to 8.

DePaola, Tommie. (1973). *Nana upstairs and Nana downstairs.* Putnam. The story of a boy who is heartbroken by the death of his great grandmother. The story continues through the death of his grandmother. For ages Preschool to 7.

Farley, Carol. (1975). *The garden is doing fine.* Atheneum. Corrie resists the impending death of her father by denying its reality. For ages 11 to 15.

Fassler, Joan. (1971). *My grandpa died today.* Behavioral Publications. A description of Grandpa sleeping away to a peaceful death in his rocking chair. For ages Preschool to 7.

Grollman, Earl. (1971). *Talking about death.* Beacon. Intended as part of a dialogue to take place between parent and child. For ages 5 and above.

Gunther, John. (1949). *Death be not proud.* Harper. The author writes of the courage of his seventeen year-old-son while facing death. For ages 12 and above.

Harris, Audrey. (1965). *Why did he die?* Lerner. A mother's heartfelt effort to speak to her child about death is portrayed. For ages Preschool to 7.

Hunter, Mollie. (1972). *A sound of chariots.* Harper. A story of a girl in Scotland during World War I and the death of her father. For ages 12 and above.

Johnson, Joy, & Johnson, Marvin. (1978). *Tell me papa.* Centering Corporation. A narrative by a beloved grandfather answers young children's questions about dying and funerals. For ages Preschool to 2nd grade.

Kantrovitz, Mildred. (1973). *When Violet died.* Parents'. The story of funeral preparations and ceremony for a dead bird. For ages Preschool to 7.

Klagsbrun, Francine. (1976). *Too young to die: Youth and suicide.* Houghton Mifflin. A comprehensive examination of a neglected societal dilemma. For ages 12 and above.

Klein, Stanley. (1975). *The final mystery.* Doubleday. Comparative religious practices, the life cycle, and humanity's fight against death are the focal points of this cross-cultural study. For ages 8 to 13.

Kuskin, Karla. (1961). *The bear who saw the spring.* Harper and Row. A story of changing seasons and the changes living things go through as they are born, live and die. For ages Preschool to 7.

Langone, John. (1972/1975). *Death is a noun.* Little, Brown & Co., Dell. Up-to-date research is the backbone of this readable examination of death's dilemmas: medical death, facing death, euthanasia, suicide, etc. For ages 12 and above.

Lee, Mildred. (1972). *Fog.* Seabury. Growing up after the death of one's father. For ages 12 to 16.

Lee, Virginia. (1972). *The magic moth.* Seabury. A mystical accounting of a young girl's death. For ages 7 to 11.

LeShan, Eda. (1976). *Learning to say goodbye: When a parent dies.* Macmillan. Offers understanding for youngsters who have suffered personal trauma. Adults who have "catch-up" grieving to do from childhood are provided with helpful ways of dealing with this problem. For ages 8 and above.

LeShan, Eda. (1972). *What makes me feel this way?* Macmillan. One gentle chapter treats death and fear of dying most assuringly. For ages 8 and above.

Lifton, Robert Jay, & Olson, Eric. (1974). *Living and dying.* Preager. Fascinating, scholarly, and intellectually demanding, this historical overview investigates responses to death through the ages, concentrating most heavily upon the present nuclear age. Primarily for the mature reader. For ages 14 and above.

Little, Jean. (1965). *Home from far.* Little, Brown & Co. Jenny and her family learn to carry on with life after the death of her twin brother in a car accident. For ages 8 to 11.

Lund, Doris. (1974). *Eric.* Lippincott. The story of a teenager's death from leukemia, told by his mother. For ages 12 to 16.

Miles, Miska. (1971). *Annie and the old one.* Little, Brown & Co. Philosophical acceptance of old age and death on an Indian reservation. For ages 5 to 9.

Orgel, Doris. (1971). *The mulberry music.* Harper and Row. Coping with the illness and death of a grandmother. For ages 7 to 11.

Rhodin, Eric. (1971). *The good greenwood.* Westminster. The story of a boy who lost his good friend. For ages 12 and above.

Segerberg, Osborn, Jr. (1976). *Living with death.* Dutton. Drawing from recent research, the author seeks to answer questions about death's mystery, the good death, and the good life which leads to it. For ages 12 and above.

Schectem, Ben. (1973). *Across the meadow.* Doubleday. The vacation of Alfred, an old cat, who leaves his home to go on a "vacation" from which he will never return. For ages Preschool to 7.

Smith, Doris B. (1973). *A taste of blackberries.* Crowell. Jamie dies of a bee sting and his best friend is confronted with grief at the loss. For ages 8 to 11.

Stein, Sarah. (1974). *About dying.* Walker. Tells of plant, animal, and human death as well as responses to death. Also explains for parents psychodynamics of loss reactions. For ages 4 to 9.

Tresselt, Alvin. (1972). *The dead tree.* Parents'. The life cycle of a tall oak tree is poetically described, showing that in nature nothing is ever wasted or completely dies. For ages Preschool to 7.

Turner, Ann. (1976). *Houses for the dead: Burial customs through the ages.* McKay. Burial rites, mourning beliefs and practices, funeral customs, ghost myths, and superstitions are discussed across time and many cultures. For ages 12 and above.

Uchida, Yoskiko. (1975). *The birthday visitor.* Scribner. A funeral needn't be a sad event, as seen in a Japanese family. For ages 5 to 8.

Viorst, Judith. (1971). *The tenth good thing about Barney.* Atheneum. Barney, a cat, has died, and his owner eulogizes him at a funeral. For ages 4 to 8.

Warburg, Sandol. (1969). *Growing time.* Houghton-Mifflin. Coping with the death of a dog and learning to understand life. For ages 6 to 9.

Whitehead, Ruth. (1971). *The mother tree.* Seabury. This is the story of a family in which the mother has died. For ages 8 to 11.

Zim, Herbert, & Bleeker, Sonia. (1970). *Life and death.* Morrow. This is an answer book for questions young people have about death. For ages 8 to 11.

Zolotow, Charlotte. (1973). *My grandson Lew.* Harper & Row. The shared remembrances between a mother and a small child of a sadly missed grandfather. For ages Preschool to 7.

RECOMMENDED READINGS
FOR PARENTS, TEACHERS, AND COUNSELORS

Bernstein, J. (1977). *Books to help children cope with separation and loss.* New York: R. R. Bowker.

Corr, C. (1980). Workshops on children and death. *Essence,* 4(1): 5-18.

Crase, D. R., & Crase, D. (1976). Helping children understand death. *Young Children,* 32 (1): 20-25.

Easson, W. (1970). *The dying child.* Springfield, IL: Charles Thomas.

Furman, E. (1974). *A child's parent dies: Studies in childhood bereavement.* New Haven, CT: Yale University Press.

Gordon, A., & Klass, D. (1979). *They need to know: How to teach children about death.* Englewood Cliffs, NJ: Prentice-Hall.

Green, B., & Irish, D. (1971). *Death education: Preparation for living.* Cambridge, MA: Schenkmay.

Grollman, E. (Ed.). (1967). *Explaining death to children.* Boston: Beacon.

Grollman, E. (1976). *Talking about death: A dialogue between parent and child.* Boston: Beacon.

Gyulay, J. (1978). *The dying child.* New York: McGraw-Hill.

Hughes, P. (1978). *Dying is different.* Mahomet, IL: Mech Mentor Education.

Jackson, E. (1965). *Telling a child about death.* New York: Hawthorn.

Kastenbaum, R. (1976). The child's understanding of death: How does it develop? In Grollman, E. (Ed.),*Explaining death to children.* Boston: Beacon Press.

LeShan, E. (1980). *Learning to say goodbye: When a parent dies.* New York: Springer.

Lonetto, R. (1980). *Children's conceptions of death.* New York: Springer.

Rodabough, T. (1980). Helping students cope with death. *Journal of Teacher Education,* 31 (6): 19-23.

Rudolph, M. (1978). *Should the children know? Encounters with death in the lives of children.* New York: Schocken Books.

Sahler, O. (1978). *The child and death.* St. Louis: C. V. Mosby.

Stanford, G., & Perry, D. (1976). *Death out of the closet: A curriculum guide to living with dying.* New York: Bantam.

Sternberg, F., & Sternberg, B. (1980). *If I die and when I do: Exploring death with young people.* Englewood Cliffs, NJ: Prentice-Hall.

Stillion, J., & Wass, H. (1979). *Children and death.* In Wass, H. (Ed.) *Dying: Facing the facts.* Washington, DC: Hemisphere.

Vlin, R. (1977). *Death and dying education.* Washington: National Education Association.

Vogel, L. (1975). *Helping a child understand death.* Philadelphia: Fortress.

Wass, H. (Ed.) (1979). *Dying: Facing the facts.* Washington, DC: Hemisphere.

Wass, H., & Corr, C. (Eds.) (1983). *Childhood and death.* Washington, DC: Hemisphere/McGraw-Hill.

Wass, H., & Corr, C. (1982). *Helping children cope with death: Guidelines and resources.* New York: Hemisphere/McGraw.

Wass, H., Corr, C., Pacholski, R., & Sanders, C. (1980). *Death education: An annotated resource guide.* Washington, DC: Hemisphere.

Wolf, A. (1958/1973). *Helping your child to understand death.* New York: Child Study.

Wolfelt, A. (1982). On being a compassionate friend. *Thanatos,* 7 (3): 18.

Wolfelt, A. (1981). *The compassionate friends: A resource manual.* Oak Brook, IL: The Compassionate Friends, Inc.

Wolfelt, A. (1981). *Filmstrip: The compassionate friends.* Oak Brook, IL: The Compassionate Friends, Inc.

Wolfelt, A. (1981). We are the compassionate friends. *Thanatos,* 6(12), 12-13.

Wolfenstein, M. (1969). *Children and the death of a president.* Glouster: Peter Smith.

Zelig, R. (1974). *Children's experience with death.* Springfield, IL: Thomas.

GENERAL TEXTS FOCUSING ON DEATH AND DYING

Beauchamp, T., & Perlin, S. (1978). *Ethical issues in death and dying.* Englewood Cliffs, NJ: Prentice-Hall.

Bugen, L. (1979). *Death and dying: Theory/research/practice.* Dubuque, IA: Wm C. Brown.

Carse, J., & Dallery, A. (1977). *Death and society: A book of readings and sources.* New York: Harcourt.

Eddy, J., & Alles, A. (1982). *A lifespan approach to death education.* St. Louis: C. V. Mosby.

Farrell, J. (1982). The dying of death: Historical perspectives. *Death Education* 6: 105-123.

Feifel, H. (Ed.). (1977). *New meanings of death.* New York: McGraw-Hill.

Fulton, R., et al. (Eds.) (1978). *Death and dying: Challenge and change.* Reading, MA: Addison-Wesley.

Kalish, R. (1981). *Death, grief, and caring relationships.* Monterey, CA: Brooks/Cole.

Kastenbaum, R. (1981). *Death, society, and human experience.* St. Louis: C. V. Mosby.

Kubler-Ross, E. (1969). *On death and dying.* New York: Macmillan.

Kubler-Ross, E. (Ed.) (1975). *Death: The final stage of growth.* Englewood Cliffs, NJ: Prentice-Hall.

Kubler-Ross, E. (1981). *Living with death and dying.* New York: Macmillan.

Kubler-Ross, E., & Warshaw, M. (1978). *To live until we say goodbye.* Englewood Cliffs, NJ: Prentice-Hall.

Levine, S. (1982). *Who dies? An investigation of conscious living and conscious dying.* Garden City, NY: Anchor Press/Doublday.

Schneidman, E. (Ed.) (1980). *Death: Current perspectives.* Palo Alto, CA: Mayfield.

Veach, R. (1976). *Death, dying, and the biological revolution.* New Haven: Yale University Press.

Wass, H. (Ed.) (1979). *Dying: Facing the facts.* Washington, DC: Hemisphere.

Wilcox, S., & Sutton, M. (Eds.). (1981). *Understanding death and dying: An interdisciplinary approach.* Palo Alto, CA: Mayfield.

GENERAL REFERENCES: JOURNAL ARTICLES

Balkin, E., Epstein, C., & Bush, D. (1976). Attitude toward classroom discussions of death and dying among urban and suburban children. *Omega: Journal of Death and Dying, 7*(2), 183-189.

Baver, H. (1976). Death and dying: A service focus for school mental health services. *Journal of Clinical Child Psychology, 5*(1), 52-54.

Bertman, S. (1979-80). The arts: A source of comfort and insight for children who are learning about death. *Omega: Journal of Death and Dying, 10*(2), 147-162.

Bowen, G. (1977). Death education with kindergarten-first grade groups. *Journal of Pediatric Psychology, 2*(2), 59-66.

Brandt, E., & Bower, P. (1975). Johnny's bird is dead and gone: Remedial work with a retarded pre-schooler. *Canada's Mental Health, 23*(2), 19-20.

Bryant, E. (1978). Teacher in crisis: A classmate is dying. *Elementary School Journal,* *78*(4), 233-241.

Carey, A. (1977). Helping the child and the family cope with death. *American Journal of Family Therapy, 5*(1), 58-63.

Crase, D. (1982). The making of a death educator. *Essence, 5*(3), 219-226.

Crase, D. R., & Crase D. (1982). Parental attitudes toward death education for young children. *Death Education, 6*(1), 61-73.

Demuth-Berg, C. (1973). Helping a child deal with a matter of life and death. *American Journal of Art Therapy, 13*(1), 39-51.

Dobson, J. (1977). Children, death, and the media. *Counseling & Values, 21*(3), 172-179.

Felner, R., Ginter, M., Boike, M., & Cowen, E. (1981). Parental death or divorce and the school adjustment of young children. *American Journal of Community Psychology, 9*(2), 181-191.

Felner, R., Stolberg, A., & Cowen, E. (1975). Crisis events and school mental health referral patterns of young children. *Journal of Consulting and Clinical Psychology, 43*(3), 305-310.

Formanek, R. (1974). When children ask about death. *Journal of Clinical Child Psychology, 3*(2), 8-10.

Frears, L., & Schneider, J. (1981). Exploring loss and grief within a holistic framework. *Personnel & Guidance Journal, 59*(6), 341-345.

Fredlund, D. (1977). Children and death from the school setting viewpoint. *Journal of School Health, 47*(9), 533-537.

Furman, E. (1978). Helping children cope with death. *Young Children, 33*(4), 25-32.

Gibson, C. (1982). Implications of an incomplete death concept and recommendations for intervention. *Ontario Psychologist, 14*(2), 20-23.

Glicken, M. (1978). The child's view of death. *Journal of Marriage and Family Counseling, 4*(2), 75-81.

Grollman, E. (1974). The way of dialogue on death between parents and children. *Religious Education, 69*(2), 198-206.

Gross, G. (1979). The child care worker's response to the death of a child. *Child Care Quarterly, 8*(1), 59-66.

Grossberg, S., & Crandall, L. (1978). Father loss and father absence in pre-school children. *Clinical Social Work Journal, 6*(2), 123-134.

Gylling, H. (1981). Bereavement therapy with an eleven-year-old boy. *Scandinavian Journal of Behavior Therapy, 10*(1), 31-47.

Hajal, F. (1977). Post-suicide grief work in family therapy. *Journal of Marriage and Family Counseling, 3*(2), 35-42.

Hart, E. (1976). Death education and mental health. *Journal of School Health, 46*(7), 407-412.

Hawener, R., & Phillips, W. (1975). The grieving child. *School Counselor, 22*(5), 347-352.

Holinger, P. (1979). Violent deaths among the young: Recent trends in suicide, homicide, and accidents. *American Journal of Psychiatry, 136*(9), 1144-1147.

Johnson, P. (1982). After a child's parent has died. *Child Psychiatry and Human Development, 12*(3), 160-170.

Kaffman, M., & Elizur, E. (1979). Children's bereavement reactions following death of the father. *International Journal of Family Therapy, 1*(3), 203-229.

Kane, B. (1979). Children's concepts of death. *Journal of Genetic Psychology, 134*(1), 141-153.

Kane, B. (1980). Unlocking death. *Early Years, 10*(5), 12-13.

Leviton, D. (1977). The scope of death education. *Death Education, 1*(1), 41-56.

Leviton, D., & Forman, E. (1974). Death education for children and youth. *Journal of Clinical Child Psychology, 3*(2), 8-10.

Lifshitz, M. (1976). Long-range effects of father's loss: The cognitive complexity of bereaved children and their school adjustment. *British Journal of Medical Psychology, 49*(2), 189-197.

Menig-Peterson, C., & McCabe, A. (1977/1978). Children talk about death. *Omega: Journal of Death and Dying, 8*(4), 305-317.

Mishne, J. (1979). Parental abandonment: A unique form of loss and narcissistic injury. *Clinical Social Work Journal, 7*(1), 15-33.

Myers, J., & Pitt, N. (1976). A consultation approach to help a school cope with the bereavement process. *Professional Psychology, 7*(4) 559-564.

Nagaraja, J. (1977). Child's reaction to death. *Child Psychiatry Quarterly, 10*(2), 24-28.

Nelson, R., Peterson, W., & Sartore, R. (1975). Issues and dialogue: Helping children to cope with death. *Elementary School Guidance & Counseling, 9*(3), 226-232.

Orbach, I., & Glaubmann, H. (1978). Suicidal, aggressive, and normal children's perception of personal and impersonal death. *Journal of Clinical Psychology, 34*(4), 850-857.

Orbach, I., & Glaubmann, H. (1979). Children's perception of death as a defensive process. *Journal of Abnormal Psychology, 88*(6), 671-674.

Parish, T., & Nunn, G. (1981). Children's self-concepts and evaluations of parents as a function of family structure and process. *Journal of Psychology, 107*(1), 105-108.

Pearse, M. (1977). The child with cancer: Impact on the family. *Journal of School Health, 47*(3), 174-179.

Rosen, H., & Cohen, H. (1981). Children's reaction to sibling loss. *Clinical Social Work Journal, 9*(3), 211-219.

Ryerson, M. (1977). Death education and counseling for children. *Elementary School Guidance and Counseling, 11*(3), 165-174.

Sartore, R. (1976). Discussing aging in school. *Childhood Education, 53*(2), 86-88.

Secundy, M. (1977). Bereavement: The role of the family physician. *Journal of the National Medical Association, 69*(9), 649-651.

Small, G., & Nicholi, A. (1982). Mass hysteria among schoolchildren: Early loss as a predisposing factor. *Archives of General Psychiatry, 39*(6), 721-724.

Smith, D. & Binge, S. (1976). Death education: An urgent need for the gifted-talented-creative whose responses to life are more sensitive. *Creative Child and Adult Quarterly, 1*(4), 209-213.

Sternlicht, M. (1980). The concept of death in preoperational retarded children. *Journal of Genetic Psychology, 137*(2), 157-164.

Stoneberg, T. (1977). Death in a family: Who's in charge. *Counseling and Values, 21*(3), 160-166.

Swain, H. (1979). Childhood views of death. *Death Education, 2*(4), 341-358.

Van-Eerdewegh, M., Bieri, M., Parrilla, R., & Clayton, P. (1982). The bereaved child. *British Journal of Psychiatry, 140*, 23-29.

Wass, H., & Shaak, J. (1976). Helping children understand death through literature. *Childhood Education, 53*(2), 80-85.

Weininger, O. (1979). Young children's concepts of dying and dead. *Psychological Reports, 44*(2), 395-407.

White, E., Elsom, B., & Prawat, R. (1978). Children's conceptions of death. *Child Development, 49*(2), 307-310.

Whitely, E. (1976). Grandma: She died. *Childhood Education, 53*(2), 77-79.

York, J., & Weinstein, S. (1980/1981). The effect of a videotape about death on bereaved children in family therapy. *Omega: Journal of Death and Dying, 11*(4), 355-361.

SELECTED PERIODICALS

Death Education. Edited by Hannelore Wass, College of Education, University of Florida, Gainesville, FL 32611.

A professional publication that focuses on a variety of topics related to death and dying. Published quarterly by Hemisphere Publishing Corporation, 1025 Vermont Ave., N.W., Washington, DC 20005.

Forum for Death Education and Counseling Newsletter. Internal publication of the Forum for Death Education and Counseling, P.O. Box 1226, Arlington, VA 22210.

Provides information/announcements regarding the Forum, brief articles, and book reviews. Published monthly.

Omega. Edited by Robert J. Kastenbaum, Gerontology and Aging Studies, Arizona State University, Tempe, AZ 85281.

An international journal for the study of death and dying. Published quarterly by Baywood Publishing Company, Farmingdale, NY 11735.

Thanatos. Edited by Elizabeth H. Peto and published quarterly by the Florida Consumer Information Bureau, Inc., P.O. Box 6009, Tallahassee, FL 32301.

Includes articles on a variety of topics related to death and dying, book reviews, and announcements.

PROFESSIONAL ORGANIZATIONS AND SUPPORT GROUPS

The Candlelighters Foundation, 2025 Eye St., N.W. Suite 1011, Washington, DC 20006.

A national organization of groups of parents of children who have had or do have cancer.

Center for Death Education and Research, 1167 Social Science Building, University of Minnesota, Minneapolis, MN 55455. Robert Fulton, Director.

Numerous professional and nontechnical publications are available, as well as audiovisual resources.

Child Study Association, 50 Madison Avenue, New York, NY 10010.

Focuses on issues related to raising healthy children. Publishes manuals, booklets, and bibliographies of reading for both adults and children.

The Compassionate Friends, Inc., P.O. Box 1347, Oak Brook, IL 60521.

A self-help organization of bereaved parents. Also has publications available on a wide variety of topics related to death and dying. The author urges bereaved parents to join the local chapter of The Compassionate Friends.

Family Service Association of America, 44 East 23rd Street, New York, NY 10010. Focuses on helping families under stress.

Foundation of Thanatology, 630 West 168th Street, New York, NY 10032.

Sponsors conferences and publishers materials focusing on death and dying.

Forum of Death Education and Counseling, Inc., P.O. Box 1226, Arlington, VA 22210.

An international organization of persons concerned with multiple issues related to death and dying. Publish a monthly newsletter.

International Order of the Golden Rule, 929 South Second Street, Springfield, IL 62704.

Provides educational materials concerning funerals, as well as death and dying.

National Council of Family Relations, 1219 University Avenue, S.E. Minneapolis, MN 55415.

An educational and referral source for families under stress.

National Funeral Directors Association, 135 West Wells Street, Milwaukee, WI 53202.

Provides educational materials concerning funerals, as well as death and dying.

National Sudden Infant Death Syndrome Foundation, 310 S. Michigan Avenue, Chicago, IL 60604.

Focuses on research and dissemination of findings. Also provides support groups for parents.

Parents Without Partners, 7910 Woodmont Avenue, Washington, DC 20014.

A group for single parents and their children. Educational and discussion groups are held. Numerous chapters are located throughout the country.

Public Affairs Pamphlets, 381 Park Avenue South, New York, NY 10016.

Provides a number of publications that focus on coping with crisis within the family.

A FINAL WORD

I sincerely hope that this book will be of value to you as you are confronted with helping children cope with grief. While working with children involved in the pain of grief is often difficult, slow, and wearing, the work also can be enriching and fulfilling. Only when we as parents, teachers, and counselors acknowledge grief for what it really is, will we be effective in our efforts to facilitate the work of grief.

INDEX

INDEX

ABOUT
THE
AUTHOR

ABOUT THE AUTHOR

Alan Wolfelt

Alan Wolfelt, doctoral fellow in the Department of Psychiatry and Psychology, Mayo Clinic, Rochester, Minnesota completed a Ph.D. in counseling psychology from Ball State University. He has lectured and conducted workshops throughout the U.S. on topics in thanatology. Historically, Alan is noted for his work in helping children cope with grief. He serves as an educational consultant to hospitals, schools, universities, and community agencies.

Alan is member of the teaching faculty of The Forum for Death Education and Counseling, and is currently serving on the Professional Advisory Board of the Foundation of Thanatology. Other memberships include the American Psychological Association and the Association to Advance Ethical Hypnosis.

He has authored a number of published articles related to the therapist's role in the grief process, children and death, and funeralization. Among his publications is the filmstrip, *The Compassionate Friends.*